"Dramatic is an understatement! Andy's life lurches from one tragic and despairing episode to another, thanks to his own folly and the devil's evil schemes. Even when he manages to keep it together on the surface, it's falling apart underneath. But God keeps hold of him and eventually Jesus Christ lifts him out of the pit and puts his feet on solid rock. Any who doubt the power of God to transform people should read this book. Andy writes with raw and vivid honesty and doesn't sell us any pat answers. His life was sadly too typical of many trapped urban young people, but his breaking free and becoming a new person in Christ proves there is hope for all."

Derek Tidball, Author and International Speaker

"Having known Andy as a child I am thrilled to see what God has done in his life. This is a gripping story of the restoration that God offers to broken people. All parents who despair over their child's rejection of God should read this and be encouraged to keep on praying."

Nick Pollard, Co-founder of Damaris Trust

"A fascinating read of a journey with God's grace at work at our extremity."

Dave Edwins, Retired Moorlands College Lecturer and CEO of Ontrack Ministries

"From sleeping on the streets, addictions, violence and being detained at Her Majesty's pleasure, to significant church ministry. How? With customary honesty and humour Andy Robinson tells his story of what God can do with one wasted life. Fast m~ ˙ ˛ and a great read."

Declan Flanagan, Chief Exec~

"We are helped by hearing p~ their circumstances. Andy R~ worth listening to – read it an~

Ian Coffey, Moorland~
MA Course Leader an

~pal (Strategy),
~f Leadership Training

"Don't read this book if you can't handle a vulnerable, shocking and disturbing story of a life lived without God. Do read this book if you are someone in the depths of darkness, wondering if there is anyone who has been there like you, addicted, lonely, destitute and yet has managed to find a genuinely better future. Do read this book if you love to read true stories of how the power of God can genuinely and authentically transform a depraved, broken, devil-spoiled life. Do read this book if you are a heartbroken Christian parent wondering if your prodigal child will ever make it home."

David Oliver, Author

"Andy is an incredible man of God, passionate in his clear, uncompromising style. The story of his life in this book feels almost unbelievable, because his journey has so often balanced on the brink of life and death. His story is breathtaking, and yet there are deep threads of grace, forgiveness and love running throughout. Today, I encourage you to delve deep into this book. It contains huge lessons for the local church today about understanding people where they are at. My respect for a man, and indeed his wife and whole family, whom have grown in their love and grace over the years. And moving forwards, Andy is passionate about sharing his story of how God's love is transformational and the wellspring of life. Andy today struggles with his physical health, but he keeps going, trusting God in all things and what a challenge for each one of us this is."

Andy Dipper, Chief Executive, Viva, Together for Children

THE CHOICE

Serving Heaven or
Serving Hell

Andy Robinson

Sovereign World

Published by Sovereign World Ltd
PO Box 784
Ellel
Lancaster
LA1 9DA
United Kingdom

www.sovereignworld.com
Twitter: @sovereignworld
Facebook: www.facebook.com/sovereignworld

ISBN: 978 1 85240 711 7

The publishers aim to produce books which will help to extend and build up the
Kingdom of God. We do not necessarily agree with every view expressed by the
authors, or with every interpretation of Scripture expressed. We expect readers to
make their own judgment in the light of their understanding of God's Word and
in an attitude of Christian love and fellowship.

Printed in the United Kingdom

Editing by Sheila Jacobs
Photography & front cover by David Lund
Cover photograph features Andy Robinson

Some of the names in this book have been changed to protect identities.

For my wife
who made the wonder of life a reality

For my three children
who show me the joy of living

For my family
who stood by me

For Locks Heath Free Church
who saw in me what I did not
And for Sherborne Community Church
who so gracefully allowed me to be their pastor

Contents

FOREWORD

The year 1812 heralded the first edition of the famous brothers Grimm's *Fairy Tales*. Sometimes stories such as Andrew Robinson's can read like one of them – a cautionary but heartening tale, like their *Hansel and Gretel*. You remember what happened to them? Abandoned to the woods at the behest of a heartless stepmother, lured to a candy house where a wicked witch intends to cook and eat them, liberated by the wit of Gretel, they finally live "happily ever after" because of the treasure they find and the father to whom they return. But the story is not *really* true. This one is!

Firstly, you are about to discover a cautionary tale indeed – sex, booze, drugs, crime, prison; occultic, dark powers; broken relationships, hopelessness, fear, overdoses and despair. It is narrated without sensationalizing, rationalizing or justifying the depths of darkness to which Andrew sunk. But unlike the resourceful Gretel, it was not his cleverness that led to his liberation. Rather, it was that grace of God (that is rightly called "amazing") that came to this lost soul's rescue.

Unlike a fairy story, however, Andrew has not simply lived "happily ever after". He is honest about his post-conversion struggles, his hard work to get a degree from this college, his battles with ill-health, and challenges in Christian ministry. This part of the story is so important to tell because it is true to what the Christian life is also about. It is not always a thirty-two teeth (or however many you have!) grin. Rather, as the Lord Jesus warns, "In this world you will have trouble." Thankfully, he adds, "But take heart! I have overcome the world" (John 16:33).

The year 1812 has another claim to fame. Although not written until 1880, Tchaikovsky's "1812 Overture" celebrates Russia's defence of its fatherland against Napoleon's invading army. Memorably, it crescendos with chimes, cannon fire, and a brass fanfare. One day, Christians believe, another piece of music will eclipse all others as it reverberates around the cosmos: "To him who sits on the throne and to the Lamb be praise and honour and glory and power, for ever and ever" (Revelation 5:13). Then we live "happily ever after", and that will be no fairy story but gospel truth. May this book help you to find out how and why.

Dr Steve Brady
Principal
Moorlands College
www.moorlands.ac.uk

INTRODUCTION

This book is not a reflection on my, or my family's, shortcomings or failings, but on the devil's. It's a book not about human differences, but about the battle for life between a God of love and Satan, the destroyer. It is not just my story, but God's. It's about understanding the mystery of God, discovered through the most painful paths and against many odds; it is the the mystery my family knew and so desperately wanted me to experience.

Our love as a family is strong enough to offer you this book with vulnerability and an honesty that says, "What we have in Christ far outweighs any mistakes, shortcomings or human frailty." Real love, true love, always wants the best, always holds out for the best whatever the price, whatever the cost, and my family have sought that for me, wanting me to have the very best life can offer – the Lord Jesus Christ. God is a God of oneness, of unity. My family has unity in God, and I praise God for them and all they mean to me.

"Behold I am making all things new"
Jesus Christ (Revelation 21:5 KJV)

This story is not exhaustive; indeed, many incidents have been left out or omitted for various reasons; and a few paragraphs may cover many months or more. I have endeavoured to share with you how I felt at the time; however, this is not necessarily the way I feel today. One of the reasons I felt I had to write this book now was because our stories don't stop; they keep going, with new chapters being lived every day. Therefore, I had to write this one before the book got too big! I have written it, too, as a response to people's requests for the whole story to be written down, after I have spoken at various events and only been able to share parts and glimpses. People always have questions and want the fuller picture. Well, here is that picture, and I hope you enjoy it; more to the point, I hope you find in it hope to inspire you that Jesus Christ is alive, loves us, and can change our lives.

Andy Robinson

Summer 2012

Chapter 1

On the Streets

The floor was so cold it pierced right through my clothes. The coldness seemed to reach right inside of me, and I understood with a brutal reality that cold really can chill you to the bone. I was sure if it was anything like the previous night it would only get colder. Being cold is fine when you know you'll eventually get warm, but when there's no chance of that it's the most demoralizing, desperate situation – and I was in it. The agony was that I *had* to sleep; I couldn't stay awake. I needed sleep to take me away from the reality of my life and the utter pain of being alive.

It was a dark October night, the sort of night where you see your breath cloud the frosty air, and I had been walking around searching for a place to sleep. I had to find the right place – safe, and if possible, sheltered. I worked my way around the usual haunts, but finding them taken I eventually gave up and headed for the high street. Southampton's large shopping centre was full of stores, pubs, clubs and restaurants, so even at night it was busy. Eventually I found a spot which was to be my camp on numerous occasions

– Moss Bros, purveyors of gentlemen's clothing. Now, I didn't pick Moss Bros because I fancied their fine clothes, but because they had a great entrance. It was the type you often see at jewellery shops. Not just a porch and front door, but a bit of a corridor which allowed people to see the merchandize on sale. I was able to get out of the biting wind, and any sleet or rain; plus, the lobby kept me sheltered but also hidden, and away from people. An added bonus was that it was right across from the large public toilets.

I used to watch the nocturnal revellers passing by, and reminisce about fun times, times when I was out on the town; when I was the one clubbing, dancing, out with the girls. I loved that scene, and it had played a big part in my life.

I knew I'd have to wait for exhaustion to come before I could sleep. The night would go so much quicker then. I needed to pass out, to be drunk or high – a powerful block, however temporary, against the pain, misery, and that mind-numbing cold. I needed a drink, sex, fags or drugs, anything to escape this world for a while. Wishful thinking, though.

Ever spent all day with someone you don't like too much? That's what it was like for me on the streets. If you've had no real contact with another human being, your mind constantly talks, discusses, thinks and wanders into unreality. As I lay there that night, I remembered walking miles that day; I'd been walking to keep my mind alert, looking for money or a load of fag ends which I could convert into new cigarettes – people never smoke right to the end. That day I'd been able to buy some Rizla papers and collected loads of cigarette butts. Nicotine – not the best quality, but it would do; that was all I wanted right now in life; just to get lost in pleasure for ten minutes. Heaven would be a bottle of Jack Daniel's, a packet of real fags and a warm bed.

I had been drunk earlier but wished I'd waited and left the

booze until now; that would have helped me sleep. Fear, too, kept me awake. I was watching out for a guy I'd met in one of Southampton's parks. During the day, the parks were all lovely beds of flowers, children playing, and office workers eating their sophisticated lunches. But when darkness fell, out came the sex addicts, those who preyed on the young and helpless; the clubbers staggering home frustrated by their lack of success at "pulling", or angry because of a missed taxi, an argument, a bouncer who kicked them out of the club; the tanked-up bullies looking for a punchbag or just to look hard in front of their girlfriends.

Last night in my wanderings I had met this man. He had seemed really nice, early to mid forties, fairly well-dressed. It was a pleasure to have someone to talk to; it turned out he was just another bloke down on his luck. But before long, I realized he was after more. He offered me his benefit money if I was prepared to have sex with him. I declined.

I'm six foot, but skinny back then, and he was a taller than me and well-built. As he grabbed me and tried to drag me off into some rose bushes, my only advantage was that he was steaming drunk and so not totally steady. As I struggled, it flashed into my mind that the roses, something so beautiful, the flowers people admired each day, were to be witnesses to something unspeakable. I tried talking, I tried pushing, but was really aware that I didn't want to make an enemy. Suddenly a guy and his girlfriend appeared on the path nearby. They evidently knew the man.

"Alright?" they said, pleasantly.

With that, the man had to appear normal, so he stopped trying to get me into the roses. It was a reprieve for me. Man, I was scared! How many more people were out there like this? How many more nights would this happen to me?

"This is crazy," I murmured to myself. "I've got qualifications.

I've been brought up well. I'm not the right sort of person to be in this position!"

But then most homeless people I met seemed to be like me; most would tell stories of times when they had wives, children, and a good job. How fine the line is between having everything and having nothing.

The evening wore on, and I began to wonder why the night seemed to evoke so many emotions. One minute it was someone crying, the alcohol-fuelled "No one loves me!" or the over-the-top "I love everybody!". Then there were the angry ones looking for a fight to show their manliness to the girl they had just picked up. There were some "normal" people, too, just out after a hard week's work. A few glanced my way; at least they weren't spitting at me tonight. Some turned their heads, embarrassed to see a fellow human being in such a state.

"You know what they say," I heard one of them mutter. "They all want to be there on the streets."

"Another piece of great wisdom by 'them', whoever 'they' are," I said, under my breath. As if trying to sleep on a hard tiled floor on a freezing autumn night was all I ever wanted!

No one stopped to talk. I wanted a conversation, I wanted a place where I needed to be, I wanted someone to miss me, I wanted someone to notice me – who I was, not *what* I was. Time after time I had the same thought: "If I died here and now it would make no difference to the world; my passing may be mourned by my family, if they found out, but no one else would miss me." Tears welled up as the loneliness engulfed me; it was more painful than the cold. My heart ached to be loved and to love someone, but I had destroyed any relationship I'd had. I'd used people. I hadn't thought about their feelings when I'd robbed them or taken advantage of their hospitality. My heart was as cold and hard as the floor I was lying on, and I guessed I deserved to be here alone. Life was empty, I had nothing; worst of all, I had no hope. There was nothing to aim for, no way I could see life changing. This was it until I died.

I was seventeen years old.

Chapter 2

In the Dock

As I lay there, I fingered the sharp point in my pocket. My knife. Not any old knife – this one had good memories attached to it. It reminded me of fishing trips, of cutting things for no reason, of whittling sticks to make spears, carving my name on trees, showing off to my mates. This knife was a cherished possession. I recalled those happier days at home. I wondered, as I often did, what my family was up to. I knew I couldn't go back. I was no longer their son, and I hated their God. I couldn't bear to live in an environment which was so claustrophobic. When I had lived at home it was like I was a saltwater fish in a freshwater pond.

I had nothing to look forward to. As I sat there talking to myself, imagining this and that, I suddenly felt an overwhelming desperation. It was weird considering I was outside, but I felt trapped. I was angry, and sick of this bitter cold. I wanted to lash out, to hit something, hard. I wanted out. Then I had an idea. My thoughts went like this: "I've got previous. The daily stealing and robbing to live means I could be a wanted man. If I was to attack someone with the knife, I'd get time. I could go to prison where I'll be warm, safe, get food and be able to sleep in a bed." The cops are wise to this sort of plan, though, so I knew it would have to be convincing. But I didn't want to get hurt. It was no good me pulling out a knife if my target pulled out a gun.

I talked to myself about my idea. No one else to talk to… only God, and I refused blank to talk to Him. He was the one who had put me in this predicament. He could have intervened and stopped all the bad stuff happening to me, so He either intended it or got a kick out of it. Therefore it was His fault.

In truth, I couldn't stand any mention of God. It conjured up images of my life at home. God took priority, and unless you followed Him, anything you said or did had little or no relevance. I spoke to the devil sometimes, but he never seemed to answer my requests, even though I thought he should because they were pretty bad and would really dishonour God.

I started thinking about my knife plan again. Doing a copper would be perfect. I didn't like them, and the evidence would be compelling; also, coppers always seemed to be tougher on people who attacked them. I knew the police patrolled the high street on a regular basis. Eventually I spotted a uniformed officer coming my way. He was alone. My heart was in my mouth. Should I stab him, had I got the guts to stab him, what if I killed him? "This isn't me," I thought. "I like people!" All this crazy stuff was going round in my head as my heart beat so fast it almost felt like the racetrack on Grand National day, pounding, galloping…

I pulled the knife out of its sheath. I knew I would lose it. I didn't have much left from home; most of my stuff was either sold or locked up in B&Bs, waiting for me to pay the rent. The knife was about seven inches long, with a hilt which would stop me getting cut if I did stab him. "How thoughtful!" I mused, as I waited.

The copper was close now; I could see him checking doors, shaking them to see if they were safe. What should I do, jump out? A cold sweat came over me. "Can I do this?" A voice inside convinced me easily: "What else are you going to do, Andy? Come on. Get yourself locked up, safe, away from the perverts, the bullies, the cold and the hunger."

I jumped up and leapt out of the shop doorway, waving the knife in the face of my enemy. He was well trained in one-to-one combat. He grabbed my arm and did one of his manoeuvres, but I had to fight, I had to be convincing. So the struggle continued, with the poor policeman thinking I really wanted to kill him and me trying to pull off an Oscar-winning performance to secure a bed for the night. Eventually back-up arrived and I was overcome.

This was one of many trips to Southampton's cells. The cops had brought me in and I went through the charge process – I had no fixed abode to give them and was less than cooperative – and I would appear in court the next day. In the meantime, I was semi-stripped, my belt was taken from my trousers, and they took my shoelaces – all designed to stop you killing yourself. I was left waiting for a solicitor; people like me who had no money or job had to have the duty one, and they would do all the legal stuff to get you out if possible. At that moment in time, that was the last thing I wanted. I didn't want freedom; I needed to convince the magistrate that I would be a menace to society if released.

My solicitor came at last. He was actually really nice and I was struck by his listening ability. He wasn't shocked by anything I told him. Later on, he was to represent me many times and play an important part in liaising between me and my parents and helping them understand criminal law. "You should get bail if I you can provide an address," he told me.

"Look," I replied, "I don't want out. I'm cold, hungry, hacked off. I want out of this lifestyle. I want to get sent down."

"I understand," he said, "but you haven't really done enough."

Hadn't I? I sat back. Right, I needed another plan. I was already facing possession of a deadly weapon, so when it came to the police interview I recalled a past crime in an attempt to cross the boundary and win a custodial sentence.

A huge glass shop window makes one heck of a smash at three in the morning when it's all so quiet. But I had had no conscience; I was with my fence, Stuart, who used to help me sell the goods I stole to make money to live. We had walked around for ages looking for a good shop to do over; in the end I found this tobacconist. It was perfect; it was not well protected, and alongside was an alley leading to a car park. The front display window was bricked up to waist height and the rest was glass. In the window were several large display cabinets full of Zippo lighters. These were really "in" towards the end of the 1980s. You weren't a proper smoker unless you had a Zippo lighter. They were brass and covered with all manner of designs.

I'd found a hefty lump of stone and stood facing the store. I was aware some people lived above the shops, but I was quite an expert at breaking windows. Speed was the priority; noise was a certainty, so I knew I had to be quick; as soon as the window shattered, the alarm would go off. As I heaved the stone, the window smashed first time. It was so loud it just echoed around the empty streets and then there was this deathly quiet. The shop wasn't alarmed.

We'd grabbed all the lighters. I had wanted more; I'd wanted to get some cigarettes, but there wasn't time. Lights were starting to come on, people were appearing at windows, and it wouldn't be long before the police turned up. It was so ironic it was crazy; there we were with our haul of fifty Zippo lighters retailing at twenty quid each, and not one fag between us to light! As dawn was fast approaching, we could not risk another smash-and-grab, so we headed back to Stuart's bedsit.

These were days of complete coldness for me. I didn't care whether I was caught, and that made me a good thief. I felt no guilt. I thought the world owed me something because I had had no luck in life.

"Anyway," I'd thought, grimly, "what can the authorities, the police, the courts do? The worst they can do is lock me up. They can't kill me."

The tobacconist's burglary, although not the crime of the century, was in the paper. The proprietor told his story of how his business was near to closure anyway, and that our actions had left him with real costs for both the window and his stock. I couldn't have cared less; he should have had insurance.

Because of the newspaper report, I knew the police would be aware of it. So I offered it up in the interview room; sort of grassed myself up, really. The police wanted the fence, too, but I just kept saying it was only me, and in the end they gave up asking and disappeared out of the room. They soon returned, this time with a list. It was the hit list of local burglaries, shop grabs and other crimes. The police obviously thought this was great; I was singing like a canary, so they could get a few jobs off their books and increase the crime-solving stats for Her Majesty!

"Did you do this one? What about the estate agents in this road?" and so the questions continued. I refused to confess to jobs I hadn't done.

I really did sleep that night. It was a stone bed and I had a rough blanket, but I was probably in the safest place in the world, locked in a seven foot square cell surrounded by policemen. Although I slept, using the loo – a slop bucket in the corner – was a nightmare and took some getting used to, especially when there were others around to share the experience with.

Next day was court day. From my previous visits, I knew I'd be put in a holding cell with others, and as usual the bragging started: "What you up for?" Well, I was up for the smash-and-grab on the tobacconist, and nineteen other cases which I had asked to be taken into consideration.

I was collected from the cell, handcuffed, led along the corridor and up the stairs to a gate. I went through and came out in the dock. A policeman stood next to me. I knew what would happen; I'd be asked for my name, address, and date of birth. My solicitor would say some stuff, the magistrate would talk with the people each side about what they could do with me, and then I'd be freed or charged and sentenced, or remanded while they did some investigating and took social reports on my circumstances.

As I stood in the dock I really didn't care any more, I wanted to go down. Life had become too hard, too much. I wanted out and prison seemed an easy life. Life had become too much effort for no gain. I heard the words "remanded in custody awaiting sentence" and I knew I was on the way down.

I was taken back to the holding cell and told, "Transport will come later to take you up to HMP Winchester." I had succeeded. I was off the streets, and I was going to get food and sleep and all the rest I wanted. I sat on the coach without a care in the world – until I saw the large gates of Winchester prison shutting behind us, and the dogs and the guards and the wire. What on earth had I done? What was this place? A cold sweat returned as I realized my freedom was gone. Even if all I did with it was walk around on the streets, I had still been free. The Grand National race was on again as my heart began to drum against my ribs. Would I ever get out of this place? I had no idea how long I would be here. A deep fear rose in my being and it was as though the devil mocked me deep in my soul. I felt tricked, conned and abused.

Suddenly, life had become very serious indeed.

CHAPTER 3

A DEAL WITH SATAN

How did I end up in Winchester prison? How come, at the age of seventeen, I had been sleeping in the doorway of some shop?

You could well be forgiven for expecting my upbringing, my home life, to have been sad, empty, drug-fuelled and violent, with parents who were absent or dysfunctional. The reality is that none of the above fits. I come from a lovely home. It was me who was not so lovely.

I was born on 13 October 1971. My brother Paul was three years older, and my brother Daniel was born two years after me. Now, I was growing up. This puberty thing hit and it was like the world changed overnight. Suddenly I wanted different stuff. Suddenly I had desires. Suddenly I needed more out of life. I knew I could get what I wanted – the fun stuff, the wild stuff, the dangerous stuff – but what seemed to be standing in the way was my family, or more to the point, their way of life – their God. *Their* God, not mine. I used to be OK with God when I was younger, but not now. I wanted the world, I wanted the good stuff, but God stood in the way of all that, and He had somehow convinced my family that they should settle for less. I, on the other hand, wanted more.

One day, in school, there was a commotion. A group of people were huddled around Debbie's prize work. Someone had scribbled across it and completely destroyed it. The whole class and teacher turned and stared at me with deep accusation as I walked into class.

"Andrew," the teacher said, sternly, "go and report to the Head."

"No."

The teacher went mad. She made me stand at the front while she whacked me with a metre rule across my hand and side. It snapped. Then I snapped.

I threw the tables and chairs around the class, the teacher huddling the kids away into the corner as if protecting them from a rabid dog. That's what I felt like – anger, frustration, because for once I didn't do this. I climbed out of the window and ran across the fields. The police found me later that day. They had been turning the neighbourhood upside down looking for me.

Not long after this, I began to smoke. I was talking to a friend and he started smoking. This was right up my street; not allowed, relaxing, smelt amazing, and oh, so cool. Once I started I never stopped and was soon addicted. At such a young age – I was about twelve – getting cigarettes would always prove difficult but I found ways, generally by stealing or reusing money given to me by Mum for my bus fare or for imaginary "school projects". At the end of the day this was my rebellion on the side; my own little way of putting two fingers up to the world. I was beginning to feel the anger and resentment building inside and the crazy thing was, I didn't really know why.

My teacher yelled at me from the front, something about concentrating. I was miles away. The classroom was on the first floor, the windows were slightly open and I was looking across the fields. I'd had enough; I didn't want to listen, so I purposely dropped my compass out of the window.

"Can I get my compass, Miss? It's fallen out the window."

"No, you did it on purpose. You'll have to wait."

"Let me get my compass, you ****!" The profanity screamed out from my mouth. "If you don't, I'll jump out the ****** window."

"Don't speak to me like that. Go and see the Headmaster," she ordered me.

But by then I was on the desk, and then I was crouching on the window frame, with the class watching, daring me – the same class that had known me jump out of windows before. I suppose they didn't quite have the nerve to say "Do it!" but probably hoped that once again the "head case Robinson" was going to make school a bit more exciting.

"Don't you dare!" shrieked the teacher.

That was as good as a push. I jumped. I landed OK, collected my compass and nonchalantly sauntered back upstairs into the classroom. The teacher, visibly shaken, had called for the Headmaster. I felt victorious. It was at this point that it occurred to me that perhaps the power of God's enemy, the devil, could be used in my favour. I felt a sense of no limits; I felt alive. However, just to be sure I *was* alive, the Head called home and insisted I was taken to the local hospital's accident and emergency ward for a check-up.

This was the start of many such incidents, either between school and me or my parents and me. It was the same scenario when the Head caught me kicking a ball over a fence on purpose. I was fine until the reprimand, the "I have authority over you" command.

"Go and get the ball back!" he demanded.

"*You* go and get the ******* ball back," I replied.

As the Head stormed towards me, I knew I was in for the slipper or maybe even the cane (which no one had ever seen). Again something snapped. Picking up a large branch from a nearby pine tree, I stood there, ready for him. Who was going to back off first? The Head did. I felt the power returning to me; I felt the authority coming to me. I gave chase. I ran after the Head, waving my stick and threatening to do all sorts.

I think this was also the trigger for a whole bout of bullying. I had a problem with my legs when I was born (I was born with a bent tibia and fibula) and had often received abuse from my peers over this defect, so I fought back. I went too far, though, and used it as a great excuse for bullying or attacking others. I wanted that power; I'd been bullied by others and I wanted payback. I wanted to do some bullying of my own. Sadly, like most bullies, you tend to pick on those you know you can beat. Funny really, the amount of times you hear people say, "Oh, he's a good kid, just in with the wrong crowd." That label fits anyone, but someone has to *be* the wrong crowd. *I* was the wrong crowd. I was possessed with anger deeper than I'd known before; the crazy thing was, I hadn't even got to secondary school yet.

After suspension and many issues with junior school, it was deemed best that I travel to a secondary school where I didn't already have a "label" or was expected to be the nightmare kid and live up to the reputation I had developed. This seemed to work. I enjoyed secondary school. I loved sports and enjoyed the challenge. But I really didn't like people telling me what to do. Whether at school or at home, it was as if everyone else just ordered my life. "Why?" I thought. "Am I that dangerous when left to my own devices?" My two brothers seemed to do OK; they appeared to have a handle on life. By that time, I knew I was the "black sheep", the problem child, the one who needed help somehow – needed fixing. But I didn't want fixing. I felt hate and resentment towards anyone who wanted to change me. I interpreted it like this: "People who tell you what to do are against you. So whenever I'm told not to do something, I will do it."

So, I was getting into some trouble, but nowhere near as much as I had when I was younger. But stuff at home was still bad. I was running away on a regular basis. I couldn't stand being around people or the demands they made. Empty, confused and angry, I just wanted to be alone.

I hooked up with some kids from the local children's home. Now, these guys seemed to have it sussed; no parents, no ties, they were expected to get in trouble, they were expected to have issues, and their curfews seemed a lot better than mine. We'd hang out together causing terror in the neighbourhood but having fun as well. We did have one problem, though. One of the boys kept getting nosebleeds every five minutes; something to do with his dad banging his head against a wall. So there was me, another guy who was really fast, and the Bleeder. If we'd just pulled off some terrifying act of vandalism or we were being chased across a builder's yard by security guards, I would run, Speedy would run, and the Bleeder would – well, bleed. It was a close friendship trio, though. I guess I never saw what those guys had been through or didn't have in life; it all looked so rosy to me.

Why was I so angry all the time? I reckoned it was the God stuff at home. It was choking me. It was all so stiflingly religious. I couldn't do anything; I couldn't play football on Sundays, I couldn't go to parties. I figured that if my parents loved God so much, that was their choice, but I was making my own choice. I was entitled to that. They wanted me to commit to God, so in keeping with what *I* wanted, I decided to commit my life to the devil, to Satan.

"That should really hack them off," I said to myself.

The weird thing was, I had recently been baptized in the family church. I had loved the idea of being centre stage and at that point thought that if I made a go of being a Christian that this might get me accepted into the family. But it didn't work.

Around that time, I was reading Christian books we had at home and came across one called *From Witchcraft to Christ* by a lady who had been a real witch, Doreen Irvine. Unfortunately, I became more interested in the exciting demonic stuff it spoke about, rather than the conversion to Christ. And it influenced my thinking.

"The devil's cool. He can provide the good stuff – invisibility, sex, orgies, power to kill things, all manner of carnal desires. Yes, I'm willing to trade my soul and all that rubbish if that's really what happens when you do these deals with him. How bad can it be? Surely it's just like praying to God, only for different stuff, and you can see it for real."

So, one night, lying on my bed, taking a deep breath, I did it. "Look, to be honest, Satan," I said, out loud, "if you can give me all the money and sex and power that I want, frankly you're welcome to any of the soul, spiritual stuff."

I was praying to Satan to take my life in exchange for the things I wanted. I prayed over and over, giving Satan a shopping list of all the things I desired, each time offering the devil more and more of me. I waited but I felt nothing. I'd been feeling nothing anyway, so no change there. I shrugged. Obviously it was like the God stuff; promised a lot, but in the reality of life, absolute pointless rubbish.

CHAPTER 4

SON FROM HELL

I was lonely. Yes, I had a family, but I was different. They had something together; they had God and each other and they seemed happy with that. But why was that not enough for me? Why didn't it make me happy? I wondered, as I often did, "Am I adopted? Why am I so different?"

I didn't realize at first, but after committing my life to Satan, things definitely got worse. My relationships with my family were getting more strained,, and my anger, my pain, my loneliness were getting worse. One day I nearly killed one of my brothers with a kitchen knife because he wound me up. All he had done was put ice down my back while I was washing the knife. I just snapped. Before I knew it, there was my brother behind the door holding it shut, shouting "Hide! Andrew's gone schitzo again, and he's got a knife!"

And then there was my dad. I kept losing it with him. We fought. He didn't want to, neither did I, but I couldn't control my feelings. Once, I smashed the table up as the family ate. Mum was crying, my brothers were bewildered and scared. But I didn't care how they felt. I didn't care how *anyone* felt. I threw bottles and chairs as the rest of the family hid from me. Then, I can't remember how, but I was in my room and my dad was holding the door closed, waiting for my rage to subside. I wrecked my room, smashing, ripping and breaking whatever I could find. The door to my room had a square glass window in it. That door stood between me and freedom. It was holding me back. My fury boiled up and I punched through the glass, smashing it over my dad. I watched emotionless as Mum picked the glass from Dad's back. Who was taking my emotions? Why didn't I feel anything? Why didn't I care?

My dad couldn't cope with the way I treated the family. He loved my mum and wanted to protect her and my brothers. I was only in my young teens but I would threaten Mum as well, scaring her. Our rows, or rather my rants, came to a head as we were having a huge row.

"Come on! I can fight you," I yelled at Dad. "Come on, if you think you're hard." Finally he broke,, and the next minute I was on the floor, my lip bleeding. For some bizarre reason I felt I'd won, but then he did something which will live with me forever. He picked me up and hugged me. Suddenly I understood his love. I pulled away. I felt respect; I could see something in my dad, I could feel something for him that I hadn't before. He *did* love and care. I wished my feelings would stay with me, but they didn't. The dark hatred, the depression, were soon back in control.

"Do you know," Mum commented one day, "I haven't seen you smile for about a year."

She thought I was on drugs, that I was taking drugs in the house. She also thought that God was the answer to everything. But I wasn't on drugs; I was smoking, drinking – Meths when I couldn't get any alcohol – and heading off each night to meet with guys across town to smash up shops and parks and hang out. I needed to be with the guys and the girls. I needed people around me who felt and thought as I did, who respected me and the choices I made.

Much later, my parents told me that around then they had found me with bits of lighters, foils, a sore face and mouth, and remembered me lying on my bed looking way out of it. Then they told me I drew a huge picture with a row of shops, and there was a pathway to lovely countryside, and a person they suspected was me running to it, shouting, "Help!"

I began to get notes from Mum, cut-outs from God books, meant to make me choose another path, but they had the opposite effect. I had made my bed with the devil; he seemed far greater, far more powerful; he wanted you to do the stuff the church freaks wanted you to stop doing. The devil had power, power to kill, power to be invisible, power to get what you wanted, to have control, to wallow in lust and greed and all that I so wanted. Why would I want God? I hated God with a passion. Oddly, I never doubted the existence of either God or Satan. But every conversation in our house had God in it and to me it seemed that this was the only way anyone showed you any interest. Conversations about church or God took precedence over everything else.

It appeared that the sole focus of my relatives was "Has the black sheep turned white yet?" It just seemed to me that the only important issue was God and the only important event had to be a church one. I felt that this God was making my family love Him more than me, and that didn't seem fair. Why did I have to be a Christian to get the "fully loved" package? I didn't feel I had much to smile about. Perhaps going away would help.

Amazingly, I wasn't all bad. I did manage, without too much conflict, to finish school and even get nine GCSEs after the school managed to convince me to stay on and do some exams. That happened because of one teacher. One day I was harassing some kid in my tutor group when my tutor (not the smallest of men) came flying down the corridor, grabbed me by the arm and dragged me into the classroom. The class knew I had a habit of attacking teachers, or just being abusive, and they were all outside the door, so he closed the blinds so they couldn't see the action. I'd done the worst thing in that tutor's eyes. He could understand issues and disputes out of class, out of the tutor group, but within the group his rules were specific: the group was sacred, you never picked on or touched anyone in your own group.

As he pulled me into the classroom, I went mad, shouting, "Who the hell do you think you are? Come on, let's do it, let's fight now!" With that he clutched me round the throat and pushed me to the back wall. "OK," he said, "if you want to fight, let's do it now. I could strangle you with one squeeze. Don't take all your home problems and attitude out on me. If you're a man, come on, then, let's see what you've got." I knew he was right, my bravado with teachers was always based on the fact that they couldn't fight back.

"Listen," he said, "you have a brain. You can leave school at Easter with nothing, and get a dead-end job or something, which will seriously hack me off after I've put so much into you these last four years. Or you can get over yourself, sit your exams and then get a dead-end job because you choose to do that, or anything else you want to do."

So I stayed on at school because of that guy; he was the only teacher I ever respected.

And now I was going away. It was all very exciting.

As a family we used to travel to the open day at Sparsholt farming college, where you could see farming in action. My favourite part was the fish and gamekeeping. This was a massive dream. I was really into fish – fishing with my older brother, Paul, or keeping tropical fish – anything fishy. I'd had one passion, to train to be a gamekeeper/fish farmer at Sparsholt agricultural college. The places were few and far between. But I remember the Head of the college coming to talk with the Head of my school and my mum and dad about the course and all that it entailed. Incredibly, I won a place on the course. I was so chuffed that finally life was starting to turn around. I was going to leave home to work in Alresford in Hampshire on a fish farm and block train at college. Life seemed to be on the up.

Being just sixteen and leaving home was not difficult for me. I presume it was not too difficult for the rest of the family, either. I was so looking forward to taking control of my own life, to having the authority and responsibility and, if I'm honest, being able to do whatever I liked whenever I liked. I could smoke, drink, have sex, I could pop pills if I wanted, I could come in at whatever hour I wanted – I could not wait.

CHAPTER 5

REJECTION

It was a tough start to working life. Fish farming was a killer. It was long hours of back-breaking work, but I loved being around the lakes and the rivers, and training in both fish husbandry and gamekeeping. It was a dream. I was able to spend my time fishing, and in the pub. I made some friends, and at last life seemed to be working out for me.

During my time at Sparsholt, although I was living away, I was still only sixteen and therefore very much still under the care of my mum and dad. I would head back to Southampton at the weekends for visits.

So I still had connections with their church, and had friends at some of the groups I occasionally attended when they did things I liked, such as football or cricket, or had a social gathering.. One thing that was always popular with me was teenage camps away. Even though I was at college, during the summer holiday I had to come home, and it was the camping season. I was excited. I was going on a camping trip.

On this occasion, it was a Christian camp in Exmouth. I liked these camps. They were a great chance to relax, do sport, meet loads of new people and maybe even have a holiday romance. I didn't think much about the content, the spiritual stuff. As it turned out, this camp wouldo be more pivotal than any before it; this one changed my life forever. A tall order for a small Christian camp at the seaside.

As I arrived and was dropped off, I met my tent leader. It was love at first sight. This person seemed to capture everything about me. But what was more surprising, what was rather amazing and unbelievable, was that she felt the same way about me. Within hours of arriving, a romance had started, a romance which would change the whole course of my life. Suddenly I was obsessed. I wanted to spend all my time with this girl, and she seemed to be happy with that.

I felt alive, on fire; I wanted to live. It felt like there was more to life than what I had; this was going to be the trip of trips. By midweek I was settling into the rhythm of holiday life. One day we had a big outing to nearby Totnes, a chance to chill out, visit the town and spend some money. We went in little groups. Most of them did the visiting and buying souvenirs and postcards, but I didn't; I came back with a bottle of Cinzano Vermouth. Well under age, I was determined to prove to myself, to the group, and to my new girlfriend, just how cool and hard I was, especially as I didn't live at home and could make my own choices. I cajoled and tried to get the others to join me. Some talked about God and how this wasn't right; some were worried about getting caught. Me, I just drank. Life was good, the drink even better, the sense of going against the grain, of being above the law, above anyone, came rushing back. I was high, I was thrilled, I was very, very sick, I was unconscious.

Panic ensued among my new friends. What an idiot I was. The ambulance came. As I came round, I realized I was in Totnes general hospital. I was shamed and embarrassed. I had a feeling my camping trip would be coming to an end. Then it dawned on me it could not end because I so wanted to be with my new girlfriend.

A compromise was reached. I could stay for the rest of the week, but I was banned from leaving the campsite. All the trips and outings down to the beach, even for barbecues and sleeping on the beach were banned for me.

I didn't notice a new sensation creeping up on me. My emotions went to extremes – jealously, suspicion. I needed to know where my girlfriend was, who she was with, who she was talking to when I was not there. These were the early days of torment. All week I fought hard to hold onto the relationship. It was my first serious "love". But she was wiser than I. What for me had become a life-changing encounter was for her a brief but enjoyable holiday romance, which possibly could continue beyond the vacation if I was nearer to her.

I was crushed. She was living in Exeter and I was living in Alresford. It was miles apart – about 125 miles. I lost my sense of reality. I didn't want to go back to college, to the fish farm, to living on my own, back to a place that wasn't this place – a place where she was, a place where something amazing had happened; a place detached from reality, the reality that I found life so difficult, the reality that at any moment I felt I could lose control, or run, or just walk away from anything steady or normal.

I was back in my room in Alresford. One blessing was that I was a lodger in the vicarage and it was a big old house, so when the vicar and his wife went out in the evenings I could creep around and explore. On one occasion I found a stash of communion wine and boxes of cigarettes. I convinced myself I would just have one packet of fags but the supply was soon dwindling.

I waited at each meal, at each encounter with the couple I lived with, for them to say, "What's going on? Where are all the cigarettes and wine?" but they said nothing. It didn't matter; my mind was elsewhere, my emotions were elsewhere, and it was not just about being in love (although I had been ringing her every night), it was something else too. The majority of the guys on the camp lived and met up and went to churches in and around Exeter. It was unbearable. For them, the camp carried on, and I was feeling more and more depressed and more alone and missing the people and the happy time I'd had at that camp.

Then there was a breakthrough.

One night, when I was on the phone to my girlfriend, she said,"We're all going to a youth camp music festival at Honiton. Why don't you come?" I couldn't wait. I was so excited, but I had a problem. I had no money, no tent, nothing. But my girlfriend said I could camp with her and her friends, so that was fine. I reckoned I had enough money for the train to get me there; I'd worry about getting back later on when I needed to. The sense of anticipation and joy as I got on that train to go back to my friends, to see my girlfriend, was huge.

I got to Honiton train station and asked where the camp was. It was miles away from the station. I started walking. I walked for hours and hours, finally turning up at the campsite. Full of expectation, I found the guys. But disaster. Another group had come and the tent was now full; sorry, there was no room for me. And my girl was with someone else. What was worse, I couldn't work out if she was with this bloke romantically or just friends with him. The way she treated me, it was as though I didn't exist in any more than an acquaintance capacity. It felt like a truck had run over me.

Here I was in the middle of nowhere, thirsty, hungry, tired and with nothing. The guys asked the owner if he had anywhere I could sleep. All he had was an old Wendy House in the garden. I cried and cried, not just because of my broken and crushed dreams but because of who I was, my own stupidity, my own gullibility, my own so needy heart that I would go to all this trouble just to find myself in more.

The evening came and all the guys huddled around the campfire. I thought I could hear my girlfriend being chatted up and enjoying the attention. But it wasn't her fault. It was me who'd gone overboard and overreacted, but I couldn't stop it; I couldn't just switch off my feelings. For the whole weekend I ate one tin of beans and drank water from the farm hose. It was the worst weekend of my life, and I still had one more problem. I was in Honiton, home was Alresford and I had no money. I managed to get a lift to the station, but I had to tell them I was OK and that I had a train ticket. What fool would come all that distance on a one-way ticket? I left Honiton, and headed for the main road. I would have to hitchhike, and I knew it would be a long and hungry journey back. It took three cars and hours of walking to get home. I walked from Winchester to Alresford, about twelve miles, for the final stretch. I couldn't believe what I'd been through and I vowed there and then never to do anything like that again.

That proved the case for at least a week.

One night, as I lay on the bed, drunk on communion wine and smoking away my ill-gotten gains with my music blaring through my old stereo, I made a decision.

"I'm going to ring my girlfriend. I'm going to get the next train and go and live in Exeter. Stuff college, stuff work. I will go to Exeter. My girlfriend will be chuffed. I'll doss with some of the guys from camp, and then get a job and just live there." I grabbed my bits and pieces, put them into a bag and rang my girlfriend.

"I'm coming down to meet up with you guys," I said, excitedly.

"When?" she asked.

"Today, or maybe tomorrow."

I didn't notice any sense of unease or lack of enthusiasm from that end of the line, but I should have done.

A friend's mother met me at Exeter station. She had agreed I could stay a few nights, which was great. I think she thought I was coming for the weekend only. We chatted, but I really wanted to see my girlfriend.

She was out.

"We'll meet up later," she had said.

When I met with her and her friends later that day, there was a coolness. I refused to believe this relationship was anything other than a meeting of souls. I played the conversion card, stressing how much I'd changed, how the love of God had transformed me, and how I just needed the love and rehabilitation of friends and their support to help me through this period as a new Christian. The next few days were difficult. My girlfriend was now more like a friend; she was distant. It was obvious to everyone that our romance at the camp had just been a fling, but my heart couldn't or wouldn't accept more rejection.

Chapter 6

Dark and Empty

After a few days, my friend's mum said I had to leave. I had nowhere to go. I wandered the streets of Exeter with nothing. I'd left it all behind – a job, a college place, a home – and I couldn't understand the idiotic logic of myself. It was as if my life was being dictated by someone else. I had long since cut God off; it wasn't Him. And my prayers to the devil didn't seem to live up to expectation, either.

At last I tried the train station. There was a chance I could sleep in the railway waiting room, only until the last train, then the guy would realize I was there and kick me out. Sure enough, that was what happened. For the first time I realized you can't be assured of life's luxuries; you're not guaranteed a warm bed and a home just because you're human. They're a gift, not a right. It dawned on me through the night that I was homeless. I had nothing. I didn't know what to do. I was scared. I didn't know this place as well as my hometown. I spent the days wandering. Then I tried to see my now ex-girlfriend at her work. She said hello and had a coffee break with me. I saw her compassion, her faith, her being nice, but she had no affection towards me. And I simply did not see that this was missing.

Finally, a local policeman, a guy who had been running the camps, offered me a place to stay. It was a major breakthrough, but the conditions of my staying with him were clear. I was a reforming character and I should be looking for work, and respect the place, and so on. I found a job quite quickly – a local fish and chip shop wanted workers and I was thrilled at the prospect of being "normal".

I was happy. I could see my friends, I was near the girl I was in love with. Things were going great, until... There's always an "until" when you're so unstable. Things can change so quickly. The college had phoned, offering me my life in Alresford back, but I didn't want to know. My new life was all I wanted. But I had cravings, I had addictions – only drink and fags, but when you've got neither and you need something you don't care about the consequences; you've just got to have them.

I started on the loose change lying around the house when the policeman had gone to work. But that was not enough, so I began taking records out of his prize record collection, a few at a time, and selling them in the shops. Before long that wasn't enough, either. Then one day, needing money so badly, and quickly, I walked into the chip shop and resigned, knowing full well my boss would give me my part pay. It was money; it meant I could drink and smoke, it meant I could be alive that day. Tomorrow would take care of itself, I figured. It was day-to-day living that mattered.

So, I was out of a job and I'd robbed the guy who had offered me Christian help. Not the wisest move, robbing a policeman. Obviously, he found out and confronted me. I felt nothing but coldness towards him, even though he had been so kind to me.

I was surprised, the next day, when my dad turned up. He had travelled miles and miles and miles to come and get me, to show me love, to bring me home. He paid the policeman all that I owed him, too. I didn't think home was a possibility. I had thought they all hated me and wanted nothing to do with me – the one who wrecked and destroyed everything. But I was wrong. The love was there, but so was the restraint. Sitting back in the family home I felt like a caged lion. It was this weird collision of two very different worlds. I couldn't breathe, I couldn't survive. It was all so normal, so nice. It was all so godly and my spirit screamed from within me, "This doesn't work. You can't stay here. It's not right. It's not you!"

I waited until the night of some big swimming gala my dad was hosting for the churches in Southampton. Dad worked as an insurance agent, and I knew there would be money in his office at home. Once he had gone out, I broke open the door to the office, which was locked, and then broke open the desk drawer. I found the money, grabbed all I could, ran to the bus stop and headed for the station. I had just burgled my own parents' house. I knew I had burnt the final bridge to home. I could never go back; they would never have me back again. I was the scum of the earth, but I felt nothing, just dead inside. No one could deny me my desires.

I was soon happy and alive again. My desire was obvious and simple and fulfilled by sitting on the train, smoking, drinking lager and heading back to Exeter. I never thought the consequence of this act would finally give my mum a nervous breakdown. The sad thing is, it would not have stopped me even if I had known.

I wandered and wandered in Exeter. Days and weeks passed. When you live like this, you fall into a weird pattern of filling days with nothing, just walking and talking to yourself. I had nowhere to go. The nights were the worst; I hated the groups of young men. I worried whether they would attack me. I was scared, cold, desperate. I'd found shelter in the rugby stands, but they were so cold and the empty stadium strangely lonely. Even the empty streets had lights and the odd person moving; at least they had deliveries. I just needed anything, really, to keep that link with life.

One night, I was slumped in a doorway and someone stopped.

"You OK?" he asked.

OK? How could I be OK? I was hungry and alone. I was sixteen! Of *course* I wasn't OK. Out of the corner of my eye I saw a broken bottle. "OK?" I thought. "I'll show you OK."

It was the top half of a coke-type bottle; the neck opening made a round, jagged weapon, but I didn't want to attack that guy. No. I ground the bottle's jagged edge into my arm and dragged it along, stopping short of my wrist. The blood flowed. I did the same on the other side. It didn't hurt; somehow it felt warm, like I was alive, that I was human, that I did exist. It was a personal thing. Then I did the same to my face. That *did* hurt. I scooped up dirt and rubbed it into my arms and face. I was a bloody, dirty mess.

I lay down. Now I wanted help; now someone would come, surely. They did – first the police, then an ambulance, then more police, who came to search for the gang of five or six youths who had attacked and beaten me. What a contrast. One minute I was sitting in squalor, a mess, dirty, cold and hungry, the next I was clean, fed, lying in a bed with white sheets, everything was warm and there were people who actually wanted to talk to me and ask if I was OK, and they wanted to get me stuff and make me better. I didn't care that they were being lied to, I didn't care that their concern was based on this scenario of a young teenager savagely attacked by a gang, when it was my own doing.

A policeman appeared at my bedside. I recognized him. Yes, it was the guy I used to call a friend; the guy I had robbed. He showed immense grace and love. There seemed to be no sense of vengeance as he talked with me. He talked about the case and asked if I was lying about the attack.

"Look," he said, "we've been talking to Southampton. Apparently you are still under a local care order. You will be sent back." The next day I was collected by a friendly social worker. She talked and talked but I didn't really listen. The long and short of it was that she would be putting me on the train back to Southampton.

On the way back, I wasn't accompanied, just told not to get off until I got there, and when I arrived I was to report to the local social services office and they would be arranging a place to stay. For once in my life I did as I was told; I trusted the system. I turned up at the offices as requested. I had questions asked of me and sat in a room for a while until the lady who had been interviewing me came back. "I'm afraid I've rung round all the hostels. They're all full and have nothing pending, either. I suggest you come back in a few months and we'll try again." That was it. That was the extent of their concern, other than a suggestion that I get a Youth Training Scheme job and then I may be able to get help with accommodation. There weren't any benefits available for under-eighteens.

Armed with such helpful advice and pastoral care I left the building, knowing I was back on the streets, only this time it would be Southampton. Something inside me had absolutely died. I didn't care; I didn't even want to go back to Exeter. I didn't really even want to bother living; what purpose would it actually serve? I had nothing and no one. I couldn't go home, I'd destroyed any remaining hope or faith my family had had in me by robbing them, and I had corrupted everything. I was beginning to think the devil really had my soul. My life seemed so dark and empty, like someone had promised me gold and it had turned to dust as I'd grabbed it.

I turned and walked the three miles into the city centre to take up
my new residence in the park, on the high street. I would join with
those others the world seemed to have forgotten.

Chapter 7

Prison

I hated Southampton, not because of the town itself, but because of what I was. I couldn't get any help, I had to survive, I had to eat, I had to have my drink and cigarettes. I had various flirtations with hostels, and centres for the homeless. I'd turn up pretending to be eighteen or nineteen and they would give me a room. But when it was time to go down to the housing benefit office then they would realize my age and send me packing. Or I would just promise rent, which would buy me a few days' grace, before they caught on and kicked me out. It was all a game which always ended up with me back on the streets.

It was during this time I caught up with some gangs that used to be called "The Townies". I would doss and hang out with them in between hostels and the like. At times these guys did not realize just how rough I was living. I even hooked up with an old girlfriend who I had used to date in my final years at school. All her mates loved being around the older guys in town causing trouble and looking tough.

I can remember my seventeeth birthday. I was in a hostel, and my dad turned up with a cake and present. I was desperate to open the cards he brought with him, looking for my nan's which might have enough money for fags. It was great to see Dad but it broke my heart, too; I so wanted him to take me home, but he couldn't. I was poison. Mum was ill and scared because of me and I would ruin everything, as I always did. Once, when I was in a hostel, a lovely couple, Nick Pollard (of the Damaris Trust) and his wife got me a TV for my room, but when I needed fags I carried that huge telly down the flights of steps all the way to the second-hand shop and sold it for a fraction of the price. There was a complete numbing of conscience because of my need.

At the end of the day, I needed money. The shops were full of stuff, so I hooked up with a young guy who was in the same boat as me. We worked out a plan – that if we robbed enough stuff we could sell it and make enough money to survive. Clothes seemed the best option. It began to work out. I'd get into shops, take items into the changing room and be out with the stolen stuff, easy. But I needed more and more expensive stuff, such as smart jackets.

We decided to adopt the "who cares" approach, so I went through the door, picked up a massive bundle off the rack and legged it, my mate trying to prevent the security guard from following me. Another way which worked was, I would put on a lovely expensive coat, then call my friend over, making a big show, saying, "Nice coat, eh?" and gradually edging nearer the door. Then I'd be off down the road and away. My mate knew people who wanted this stuff; better still, he had specific orders for the items they wanted.

I now had some money to survive on. But the nights were getting worse. That's where we started this story, me in a shop doorway trying to sleep, but at the end of my tether.

The nights were bad because of the perverts, the evil that came out, because of the cold, because of the unknown, because you had to sleep somewhere and that meant being vulnerable; you can't sleep with your eyes open. As I sat there talking to myself, imagining this and that, I suddenly felt this overwhelming claustrophobic desperation. I wanted out. If I was to, say, attack someone with the knife I'd get time, I could go to prison where I'd be warm, safe, get food and be able to sleep in a bed...

And now here I was. The gates of Winchester prison were shutting behind us, and I noticed the dogs and the guards and the wire.

As we were led into the building beyond the heavy gates, I realized this world was different. This was the world of absolute authority, where someone like me, who couldn't stand authority and demands, was well and truly stuffed. This place was about order and discipline and doing this and that on time and in a certain way. I was partly scared and partly overwhelmed. This was real life, this was serious. I'd always thought, "What's the worse that can happen? They can't kill you." The streets and now prison were changing that perception. Here, as on the streets, that *could* happen. The air was full of desolation, of violence, of anger, of frustration.

For many it seemed to be return trips; they'd had some time on the outside and were back to catch up with old friends. I swore there and then I would never come back. I had to strip, then I was checked by a doctor, washed, and given my clothes. After that, I was taken to meet my new cellmate, a guy from Portsmouth. I couldn't believe it; they didn't even separate the Portsmouth and Southampton guys – two rival factions. As we went out onto the exercise yard it became more obvious. At one end were the guys from Portsmouth, at the other, the Southampton boys, and in the middle was no man's land. A horrendous tension filled the air. Just a cross word or glance would be the spark to start a fire. This place was like that, it was life on a knife edge. You had to be, or at least appear, tough, even if you weren't, or you became food for everyone else. People lost it in this place. I watched as one massive guy went mad, lost his head. It took all the screws (prison guards) to get into his cell and bury him in mattresses to get the guy out. He was ranting and raving. Another young guy just cried all the time. He didn't last five minutes before he was abused.

As the days unfolded, I realized not much was going to happen. I would be doing pretty much what I'd been doing on the streets, but without one distinct benefit – freedom. It's one of those commodities, like trust, we don't appreciate until it's gone, then we crave it with all our heart.

One day I noticed my friend looking sad and afraid. His cell was two doors' down the corridor from mine. Another bloke walked up and into his cell, then another guy walked past and shut the door on them. Fight time. No school antics, all shouting and yelling, waiting for it to be broken up; it was in quiet, in a locked cell, between the two guys only.

"This is my mate," I thought. "What do I do?"

But a guard came. He knew the score, the door was opened, and both guys emerged battered but alive.

The weeks and months passed by. I visited court periodically to catch up on my case. I remember my dad coming to court on one of these occasions. I couldn't get out unless I had an address, somewhere to go. Dad explained that Mum was too afraid to have me at home; it wouldn't work. I understood. Who would want me around? I was on my own. Finally, the court decided I was to be bailed to a bail hostel in Fareham where I was to follow strict rules and curfews. I knew as I left the court that I was never ever going back inside. It was the worst place ever. The bail house was OK. At least we had freedom to go about and do what we wanted. I headed straight back to Southampton to catch up with my friends and my girlfriend. It had been a while and I really wanted to see everyone.

We met up and chatted. My girlfriend and all her mates had written to me and so I'd kept in contact with everyone. There seemed to be some kudos in her having an older boyfriend on the "inside". It was nice to come out, though, and have someone to see. Many don't.

I went to my girl's house. I knew I had a curfew but I didn't want to go back. I considered absconding but I had second thoughts. "No," I said to myself. "I'll go back. I should just catch the train and make the curfew if I'm lucky, and anyway, they can't be that tough about it."

As I walked up to the bail hostel a few hours late, two policemen and a car were already there. In my mind I thought, "Run!" but I was convinced I could talk my way out of this one. I was very wrong. There was no leniency. I was back in custody, back in court the next day and, by the afternoon, back in the very cell I'd just left, same cellmate, same guards. Even they couldn't believe it; most people wait more than forty-eight hours before coming back inside. So much for my promise to never come back. I hadn't lasted five minutes.

VT0684 Robinson was back and I was there now to wait for my sentencing. I had been convicted, and shared the wing with the other convicted guys – some sentenced while others, like me, were waiting to know their fate. I remember meeting an old friend; on his door was the word "Life". He was in for murder; a bar fight gone wrong and that was it, life was over for his victim, and for him. That was the trouble with this place; so much wasted life, so much hatred, so much rubbish. I hated the sorrow. At night I would lay there and listen to the horrible sounds of people screaming at the nonces (the sex offenders) about what they were going to do if they got hold of them. Big men would quietly cry; big men with no hope, and shattered dreams. It was a place of pain.

One day I had a visit from a probation officer. He had to inform me that my mum was ill and was in hospital, but that it was not life-threatening. That was it. No call, no more information, back to the cell. I didn't know what had happened. I wouldn't until my dad visited. And then I found out that this information wasn't even true. Mum was ill, yes, but not in hospital.

I remember getting a letter from one of my brothers, which meant a lot. He still cared, he still wanted to be in contact. I felt hope that I had family, that maybe one day I would live in harmony, in peace with them, that somehow they might understand me, and me them. But I was so mixed up. I wanted to see my family but hated the fact they came to visit with no money or cigarettes like the other visitors. This consumed me. It was how I reacted to people; I would burn inside with rage and anger at anything. I had wanted cigarettes or money because inside it was like gold dust; it made the hell hole a bit more bearable. It was about this time that the daddy (or top dog) of the wing seemed to take an interest in me. He wanted stuff, cigarettes, all I had. At night he would shout, "Robinson, are you going to give me what you've got, or am I going to have to take it?" I knew an encounter with him would be a dangerous one. He had nothing to lose, he was in for the foreseeable future. I avoided the questions and he got angrier. I had to make a decision: give in and then be forever at his beck and call, or fight, stand up and say no.

I said, "I can't. I ain't got nothing."

That didn't work. So I said, plainly and firmly, "No."

I had made my choice. The next time we met I knew it would be bad.

Thankfully that meeting never happened. My court date came through. I think the fear of confrontation with this guy helped convince me, I either had to walk away and change, or accept this life completely and be prepared, like some of the other guys, to just spend my whole life in and out of prison. I decided never again.

In the bus going down the motorway to Southampton, I wondered what the other drivers were doing, where they were going, and did they realize they were following a bus full of criminals, all handcuffed together? As I stood and was sentenced, I was given six months, and two years' probation. I'd already done the time and would just need to spend the next two years with a probation officer, but at least I was free. But I still had nowhere to go, no job, nothing; being inside hadn't changed that, and it was not very likely to help me get employment, either.

Chapter 8

On the Up

I can remember my first night out. I bought a tin of tobacco and just smoked and watched the sky. It was enough to know that I could go anywhere, and that if I wanted, I could use the toilet. In Winchester at the time I was in there, we had a bucket in the corner of a joint cell.

Being on probation meant one good thing, they found me a place to live. There was a local landlord who seemed willing to take all manner of people into his bedsits.

The house I entered was a place of unbelievable corruption and depravity. Yes, it was warm, and there was food. But it was a viper's nest. I spoke to an old man on the top floor. I thought he was mad. Across his floor was sprinkled talcum powder: "It's so they don't get me at night. It's so I know when people have been in my room," he said. For all us guys under eighteen, we had no way of paying rent, and the probation service was meant to sort that out. But the landlord was either pimping the guys out or just keeping them for himself. It was that or the streets. The place was evil. At night I would lay and wait. I could hear fights. I could hear stuff I didn't want to hear; the pain and torment of abuse and of sorrow.

I was sharing a room with my friend Danny. We would spend our time sniffing glue, pinching cards from people, or stealing money from cash machines to buy gas and to pay for the slot machines. We would spend much time together, talking. I knew my friend had been badly abused. He would offer to sleep in my room, even in my bed, if it meant we could be safer at nights. Danny was so messed up, so corrupted, he didn't know what he was doing or who he was. Later that year, he was caught stealing a car. We shared the same probation officer, and he told me how Danny had given up. He had been found hanging by a rope inside Winchester prison. Once again I felt alone, that everyone and everything was corrupt, that you could trust no one; life was to be lived alone.

Even though it was difficult, I was in occasional contact with Mum and Dad, and their church was close to where I was living. One day some great news came through of a possible place at the hostel which the church was running, not far away. I was so excited; this could mean a new start. The landlord where I was kept everyone under strict manipulation and control with both occult and sexual bondage; getting out was hard. But it was soon arranged, and with great joy I moved into my new room in Alpha House. It was like heaven – a room and a roommate. Phil was a great guy who worked part-time at the hostel and the rest of the time with his church. Phil only had one working arm; he had suffered a serious motor cycle accident and had been left for dead. He had rebuilt his life and told me God had a lot to do with it.

As I got to know him, Phil introduced me to more of his friends from the local church and we used to have great times out. Then the most bizarre of circumstances arose. It transpired that my dad had worked for years with Phil's mum; in fact, my dad had taken

Phil to some of his hospital appointments. It was like "fate" had brought us together.

Great as it was, I was struggling to hold on to reality. I was going through jobs like no one's business; I kept finding work then hating it, or walking out because I couldn't cope, or suddenly I would feel as if I didn't want to live any more. It was like I was being pushed down this path that would inevitability end in my death. I knew it, I could feel it, and I couldn't stop it. The depression became stronger, the rejection, the hurts, the waste of space that I was, all flooded in. Who was I kidding, I would never amount to anything. I couldn't hold down work, I couldn't feel anything for anyone, I wasn't capable of love.

I became more and more depressed and withdrawn until I reached the point where I sat on my bed with the worst dilemma anyone can face: "What will hurt more, dying or staying alive?" I decided the pain of living would last much longer than the pain of death. God seemed irrelevant so I wasn't fussed about facing Him.

I waited until Phil went off to work, knowing he was the only other one who had a key to the room. I took dozens of pills, and laid back on the bed waiting for some peace, for life to finally shut up and leave me alone, for the sorrow and agony and constant struggle to live to end. I was soon asleep and out of it.

But Phil had forgotten something he needed. He returned to the room, unlocked it and found me unconscious with empty tablet boxes on the bed. He called for an ambulance, but I don't remember any of it. I was told afterwards they had managed to restart my heart, to get me breathing again, to neutralize the tablets, to clear my stomach out. I don't know how they brought me back, but they did. Phil's timely return had saved the day.

The trouble was, I wasn't thankful. How could I be? If you had any idea how much courage, how much determination and just how bad you have to be to get to that point, being brought back is making you start all over again. The problems are not gone just because you've been saved. It's all still there, plus a dose of embarrassment and humiliation as everyone gets to hear how you nearly topped yourself.

With Phil and other friends and my brother Paul's help, I did start to recover. Over time, as life continued, I was allowed to stay at the hostel even though I had breached the rules. Phil and his friends from church helped me see small reasons for living, such as a fat-filled bacon roll with brown sauce from a greasy café and decent tea over a chat on a Saturday morning!

As time passed, I managed to secure a job working in an office, and I quite enjoyed it. It was the first stable period of life I'd known. I was enjoying getting to know friends and working for a living. I moved out of the hostel with Phil into a friend's house. All was going well; so well that nearly a year early, my probation officer commented that with such good progress I should soon be taken off probation.

That year I changed jobs. I saw an advert for an ex-offender scheme to train in engineering as a draughtsman. This was amazing. I loved drawing, and this job seemed beyond belief. They actually paid you to learn to draw buildings and structures – it was awesome. I was in the best job ever, I loved the people and it seemed as if life was on the up.

Phil suggested I get involved with a church group in Southampton, and for a brief while I did. But it was not me; they all had life sorted and shiny and it was all too easy. Real life wasn't like that. I tried, but I still hated God too much to even be in a church environment.

One evening I went with Phil to a church meeting. This guy was praying for people. Some were falling down, and others laughing as the Spirit of God came upon them. The man prayed for me and said, "God says He will never let you go." I was outraged. I wanted to smack the bloke. I had to use all my power to stop myself.

God would never let me go? How *dare* he say that? "Your God does not have me! He does not have me so He can't hold onto me. He can't let me go because He will never own me!" I yelled. I was so angry. How dare God be so presumptuous – and this preacher guy too!

Before long, money reared its ugly head and I was really struggling to survive. I was seeing a married woman who worked in the accounting department of the company that employed me, and convinced her to advance my salary well before it was due. I was on such little money, but still struggling with all my old habits.

It wasn't long before I found a solution. My landlord had cupboards full of old papers, and with them I found chequebooks. These being the days when a chequebook even without a card meant cash, I realized I could scam them and steal money from my landlord. It was that old habit of needing more money, not having enough and not looking at the consequences of my actions. I was taking his cheques to the shop, old ones, and cashing them. By the time his statement came though I was hundreds up and he was hundreds down. Not surprisingly, I was booted out of my lodgings, but worse than that, I lost contact with one of the best friends I ever had and all the new relationships I'd made. I still wonder what happened to Phil and his wife.

Once again I was on my own, once again I had messed up, once again I had destroyed all I had. I was facing the road back down, but this time I had a new determination. I had more to lose than before. I was desperate to keep my job and my friends there. I turned to the company, to my chief draughtsman, to see if they could help me find a place to live, and they did.

I wish I'd owned a camera to take a picture of the place I was offered. It was beyond belief. My boss kept asking, "Are you sure you want to live here?" It was a squalid bedsit, a tiny room with a dirty curtain, behind which were a cooker and fridge. The whole place was probably twelve foot by twelve foot, and had not seen cleaning fluid of any kind for some while. But it was mine. I was amazed; I could not believe that I would have an address, that I would have my own place. Not that long ago I was lying in a shop doorway; it wasn't that long ago I was lying in hospital, unconscious; here, suddenly, was the start of real life. I had a great job and a place of my own. Life was on the up.

CHAPTER 9

NORMAL LIFE

Life was getting so good. Not only was I galloping through my apprenticeship, and loving every minute of training both as a draughtsman on a drawing board and also on computer systems, but I was finding time to enjoy myself outside of work. I loved clubbing.

It was during one of these outings that I met my wife. I had been going out with one of her friends, but she put love before friendship and we started dating. Drink and my lack of self-control were still huge problems for me. My new girlfriend knew what I was like, but that didn't seem to put her off. I would drink until I collapsed. Many a time I would be thrown out of a club then return the next night and be admitted after apologizing.

One night, at a club where I knew the staff and had been a regular for years, they had a new guy working at the bar. I had been drinking steadily for hours. The new guy was doing something else, so when I wanted another drink, he was too busy to get it for me.

I said, "I'll get my own."

He went mad. "Don't you dare!"

Saying that was a huge mistake. I was up and over the bar. He pushed the panic button and the bouncers steamed in. I fought with the barman, the bouncers and anyone else who joined in. I couldn't back down once I started. Eventually the bouncers got hold of me, two at the front, two on my legs, and carried me up the stairs to street level, where they threw me out through the fire door. I crashed at the feet of the policemen who had been called to sort it out. Another fight ensued. Eventually I was bound and in the back of the police van, down to the cells to sober up, then back home and working the next day! It was a bizarre existence.

My girlfriend didn't seem to mind my antics. I was eighteen, she was seventeen, and before long we decided to get engaged. Her family were horrified at my place and refused to allow me to go back there, apart from to collect my stuff, put the top back on the electric meter and give notice to the landlord that I was off. So, I moved in with my girlfriend and her family. They treated me well, but I was not used to families that do absolutely everything together and that was hard. Still, it was nice to be part of a family where I felt I could just be my rather odd self rather than be what others thought I should be. No one said anything if I was drunk, smoking fags or dope. As far as they were concerned, I worked hard and could play hard.

My girlfriend and I moved out and got our own place, but soon returned due to money problems. In 1992, just before my twenty-first birthday, we got married. I don't know why. It just seemed the thing to do. I remember talking to my mum and showing her that I had rebuilt my life but there was this whole thing of not being "right before God" because we were living in sin, not married, and that hurt me. Anyway, it was a good chance for a knees-up. But even as I walked down the aisle I remember thinking, "This won't last." I don't know if she felt the same. Someone had said we were too young to be getting married, but we said our vows and it was a great day.

We didn't start well. We were both on training schemes, so had little money. We moved in and out of rental accommodation, struggling all the time. We ended up back at her mum's house. It was not the best place to be, but not long after we moved in our son was born, and we asked for a council flat. The only way we could get one was for my wife and son to live at her mum's and me to live elsewhere while we waited. Sadly, the only place I could go was back to the landlord who was manipulating and controlling, the one who had people in bondage. I hated that guy.

Finally, after a long wait, we moved into a flat in town, but it was bad. Still, I was chuffed. I was in a far better place than I had been. I had made it. I had a job, I had married, and now I had a baby boy. It dawned on me that *I* had done this stuff, that all that rubbish I'd heard from Christians about life not working without God was just not true. Here was the living proof. I was happy, I had a normal life, I had become a civilized member of society, and all without God, thank you very much.

My son was just two years old when the trouble started. My wife wanted to go out a lot, and I didn't want to go with her. The relationship had changed and we were growing apart. I was happy being home and together, but she wanted more. I was oblivious to the cracks fast appearing in my "normal life". Then one day I got the phone bill, and there was this number I didn't recognize called three or four times a day. Then she started going out all the time, all dressed up and, so I found out later, using our friends as decoys. It wasn't long before I discovered the painful truth, she was having an affair. It hurt, and suddenly I really cared, but it was too late. Whether it was my inability to relate to people, having spent so long alone, whether we were just too young, or maybe it was the pressure of living and loving in poverty – whatever, something had gone severely wrong. I confronted my wife, but she convinced me that this was all my imagination.

Then one horrendous day, as I was driving with my son in Southampton, he started talking. Still very young, he didn't speak much, but what he did say on that occasion was, "Are we going to Neil's?" He knew where "Neil's" was and how to get there. I felt awful, quizzing my little boy about the things his mum was doing, and all with my son in tow. It was devastating. I knew then that he'd been going to "Neil's" during the day, and surely no mother takes her son along while she's with a man unless it's serious. I knew at this point that my marriage was over. I was filled with rage, but at the same time I couldn't react. I had no fight left. I was too crushed.

After a huge row, the truth came out. She had fallen head over heels for this guy. I needed to know everything. It was the worst of situations; I wanted to know nothing about it, but I had to know everything, every painful detail. It was the only way to stop my mind making its own assessments and versions of the story – as if they would be any worse than the reality itself. If this guy was at least a rich, successful, handsome businessman or something that would help. But he wasn't. He was living in a dump even worse than ours. That crushed me; it crushed my whole sense of well-being, of balance, of security in who I was. I felt like I had been completely and utterly rejected and was heading back to the lowest place of all. I couldn't believe that I had fought to drag myself up to a successful, real, and normal level of life, and even that was not enough. I felt like it was me. I couldn't get normal, I couldn't be normal; life or God or someone wouldn't let me have a normal, happy existence. After getting out of the gutter, I was back there again.

The pain just got worse. We tried to make it work, because we had a child. But she was obsessed with this guy. It was eating me alive that I couldn't be as important, even with a wedding ring and a child. Inside, the love was being replaced by a growing hatred and anger, both at the situation and my inability to just walk away forever and not look back. That's what I wanted to do; that's how I usually dealt with this sort of thing. The situation was made worse by the man's family ringing me to tell me to let her go.

In the end, it couldn't go on. I filed for divorce. However, because of the way legal aid worked, my wife had to be the one filing for divorce. She needed grounds to make it go through as quickly as possible and with the least cost. So we agreed that I would put down a recent brief encounter I'd had (after the marriage break-up) as grounds for divorce – my unfaithfulness. I really didn't care. I just wanted it all to be over and the pain and hurting to go away.

I had no option really but to let my now ex-wife and son back into the flat we had had together. It was my son's home; the place he knew. It wasn't long before her guy had moved in. My heart couldn't stand the pain, the pain of wanting to see my son, to keep up the relationship with him. That meant going to collect him, to collect my own son from my own house from my wife. I would knock on the door and *he* always answered. He would then tell me when to bring my son back. As a man I can't think of a worse situation – to have to collect your own child from the new man, living in your house. Suddenly this new guy was seeing my son all day every day; he was there in the morning, he was there when he cried, when he laughed, he was the one being involved, not me. It tore me apart. All I got was a small glimpse for a few hours each week, and then my son had to go back, to go away. It was like losing my child over and over again, week after week. He would hang onto me – "Daddy, don't take me back, Daddy stay, Daddy, Daddy" – I can understand how some people just drive off with their kids. The times my heart broke and I didn't want to let him go back. I wanted to share all his life, he was my son too. I resisted the urge to just take him and drive.

I was drinking and smoking heavily again. I had to blot out the horrendous feelings of broken trust, of betrayal, of feeling completely and utterly rejected and good for nothing. I reacted not by hiding away but by going out, sleeping around, drinking and wandering round the town all night. Anything not to be alone and face the reality of life.

During one of my trips out I met another woman. She was much older than me and had a young daughter about five years of age. At the time my son was two or three and we seemed to really hit it off. She had had a terrible life and had suffered really badly at the hands of a stalker. I felt we really connected. In reality I was on the rebound, full of myself, of my own selfish ambition, and in some way desperate to put back in place what I'd lost – not just a female companion and a child as well, but I needed to feel a man again, to feel wanted, to feel that I had a part to play. I wanted to feel that I had "arrived", that I had happiness, that it was true and real and not me pretending to feel something I didn't.

This was a tough relationship from the start, but it wasn't long before we moved in together, sharing a house. I remember thinking, "This is crazy. I don't want this… but I do." I was mixed up and struggling to keep on top of my emotions.

During these times of upheaval the one saving element for me was work. I'd sailed through my apprenticeship and was working as a freelance structural draughtsman. I loved my work with a passion, and was starting to really find my way and build a good reputation in the industry. I loved being given a blank sheet or screen and filling it with a drawing which could then be built into amazing buildings anywhere in the world. It was great. But outside of work I was far from normal. I was struggling more and more with my feelings, with constant headaches and seeing things that weren't there.

It all came to a head one morning. My girlfriend came to see why I hadn't gone to work, and found me sat by the garden pond rocking back and forth, completely oblivious to all around me. The doctors explained that I'd had a nervous breakdown and that I needed rest and time and some help to overcome the recent traumas. This made me feel even worse. I couldn't even handle a bit of depression. Also, I felt stuck in the relationship because of my health. I felt such a horrendous person, that I was not being fair and honest to the woman I was living with, or her daughter.

One day I felt I just had to get out, so I went to the pub, met some girl, and that convinced me I was bad, that I needed to get away from my girlfriend. I couldn't go home now – this girl had marked my neck! So I drove, I saw stuff, I felt the closing paranoia. This was worse, this was evil, the pictures and thoughts racing through my head; it was as if my mind was being used by something else. And the pain – I wanted to scream, I wanted it to stop. It was terrifying, like I was hollow, empty, as if my life had been taken over by someone else and smashed repeatedly against rocks. I could do nothing, because it was as if I had given it away; it wasn't *my* life any more. The fear and panic was immense .

I drove, somehow, to Southampton hospital and tried to explain what was going on. They took me straight in. They seemed shocked that I'd driven there. I didn't share their concern; that was the least of my worries. I needed them to see what was happening in my head. They had to see before it took over and there was none of me left. I wanted to roll over and die, to sleep, to close down, but my mind didn't – or whatever was controlling my mind didn't.

I was taken across town to the other hospital in Southampton, and a nurse led me into a building block. It said stuff about mental health on the door, and as we walked up two floors I suddenly realized the doors were locking behind me.

I turned to the nurse. "I'm not nuts. I'm OK, it's just I don't know what's happening in my head."

"Look," said the nurse, kindly, "it's just standard procedure. Everyone is locked in, even the staff. It's to help those that are worse than you."

Really? In my heart I didn't believe it, but I was too tired to care. I couldn't think for myself any more, it was all too painful. I just wanted to turn off the lights and sleep forever. The thing was, the poor woman I was living with had no idea why I hadn't come home. She didn't know how I was feeling or whether I was dead or alive. I asked the staff to ring her but to say, "Please wait for me to ring before coming to visit." I didn't want to see her.

Later, I saw her in the ward, bringing stuff or getting feedback from doctors, I don't know which; I got the idea that there was a lot going on behind the scenes I didn't know about. But perhaps that was just the paranoia.

I wasn't there long. I was released under the watchful eye of my doctor, and had to visit and spend time with a psychiatrist. I returned home but it had become very clear that this relationship wasn't going to work out. I'd become so hard and angry. I felt the world had robbed me, that it owed me and that I was entitled to live and act as I desired. On the other hand, she had so many emotional scars we were both walking on a knife edge; the relationship had no chance.

I wanted to make up for the lost time in prison and on the streets when I had nothing. I felt that now was my time. I decided I didn't want to be in any relationship; I didn't need anyone, and people only hurt you. I was determined to go it alone, to do what I wanted and stuff everyone else. I spent some time with the psychiatrist who diagnosed bleeding temporal lobes. He basically blamed an upbringing of heavy religious bondage that had taught me to repress all my emotions, that as a Christian it was not right to feel hate, lust, fear, jealously and so on, and that learning this repression in a church environment had caused me to have mini explosions when all these feelings came to a head from time to time. I didn't believe a word of what he said but I agreed with his conclusions that I was a victim, and took the treatments so he could sign me off. In truth, I said whatever he wanted to hear. I saw it as a complete waste of time, but one that seemed important for me to go along with so that I could stay out of the hospital.

He used to give me pills. It seemed as if he had more control of me than I had of myself and I felt like he was just someone else trying to live my life, to control and manipulate me. In short, he was doing what I was afraid everyone was trying to do, capture me and then take my life. I was totally paranoid. The bottom line was, I was drinking loads, taking heavy medication, dope or anything else that became available. I was convincing myself that my broken marriage and the relationship with my son – plus another broken relationship – was all under control. Add to that the mental overload and ever-fading sense of reality… I was a mess, a real mess. The trouble was, I'd used so much fight to move up and out of each situation, I was exhausted. It felt like life would always be a fight. Every day would be a fight, a battle for money to survive, a battle to be happy, a battle to keep a relationship, a battle to trust people again, a battle to keep my job, and on and on. Life just seemed sheer exhaustion and I couldn't understand why anyone would want to play the game.

CHAPTER 10

NOWHERE TO GO

I'd moved out of my girlfriend's house and back to my old landlord's. He was still up to no good, but at least my age and big build meant I was not as vulnerable as before. All he wanted from me was my rent money.

I was working as a draughtsman for a company in Andover on prestigious projects, including the Treasury and number eleven Downing Street. I was doing well at work; it was just the rest of my life that was the problem.

During this time my ex-wife and her partner decided they no longer wanted the flat and that I could have it back if I wanted. That felt great at first, but being alone in the very place which held all my pain meant I was constantly surrounded by the very thing which was killing me. There seemed no escape. Every inch of that flat brimmed with memories, and as I walked into my own child's room, the place I'd played with him, the place I'd comforted him, the place I'd watched over him as he slept, I cried and cried. How could it be legal for people to take away someone I loved so much?

How could it be right that another man could just come and take over my most beloved possession, my son?

In the end, I shut the door to my son's bedroom. I couldn't bear going in there, it was too painful. Being alone in the flat gave me space to do whatever I wanted, and I started on a campaign of heavy drinking and self-destruction in order to escape any sense of reality or life's demands.

One good thing about being back in that area was that I had friends there, so I didn't feel totally isolated. It was a deprived area; needles and bottles and urine filled the stairwells in the block of flats where I lived, and the man who used to live below me was in prison for rampaging with an axe. Every night two black cars rolled onto the estate with the regularity of an ice cream van and everyone would get their drug supplies. Then ten minutes later the police would follow, as if to make sure they never crossed paths. But for all its rundown ragged buildings there was a real sense of community, and people did get to know each other, and helped one another.

I had people's sympathy because of my family situation. One friend, Marie, was particularly close. She lived round the corner and had been my wife's best friend, but had not agreed with the whole affair. It was lovely to have someone on my side, and her little girl was the same age as my son. It was great to have a friend who understood, but this also triggered something. I had an idea; I saw an opportunity. Something of a vengeful spirit stirred in me. I wanted to take back all that had been taken from me. I vowed to find all my ex-wife's friends and sleep with them and then turn them against her, to make her pay for the cruel way she'd stolen my life.

Marie, and I had become very good friends indeed. We would often go out clubbing together with other friends. Marie had a partner, Pete. They had been together for years and I became firm friends with him, too, but he was an alcoholic. Eventually Marie had to leave him, for her safety and the safety of her child. It was tough; these were my two closest friends, and I was in the middle. I loved them both, they had helped me during such a dark time. I couldn't understand; I drunk just as much more often than Pete, so why did he become the alcoholic, not me? I even have alcoholism in my family – my granddad died an alcoholic and my dad always warned me he could sense how easy it would be to start drinking and not stop. Pete was in a bad way. Marie tried to keep up visiting him, but his focus became the drink alone. Shockingly, my friend Pete was discovered dead in his little flat in Southampton surrounded by aftershave bottles that he'd tried to get his last drink from. He was thirty years old.

I was shattered. Another of my friends had died, too. When was my turn? It didn't seem right; how had I escaped and survived, but my two friends had not? The funeral was awful for the family, the friends, all still so young. This was a waste, the funeral of a life wasted; the service was meaningless. There was a vain attempt by people to say positive stuff about Pete, but all of us knew the reality was he'd left his wife and child to suffer while he'd pursued the drink. The minister spoke of grace and mercy, words to try to cover the situation, but we all knew the truth. Here was a life messed up. No one had much good to say, but they went through the whole process anyway, whether to please God or the relatives, I don't know, but it seemed to me he was at least free from torment, the pain of living; suicide by bottle, I guess.

Sometime after this, I realized why the flat was offered so freely to me. My ex-wife and her new man had not been paying the rent or much else, and the bills and demands were coming through the door like crazy. Instead of dealing with the problem, I drank more, worked harder and hoped it would all just go away, not that it mattered that much. I didn't have any responsibilities; my son wasn't mine any more; it felt like he was a guest I was allowed to see every now and then. I had no life, the girlfriends came and went, one night stand after one night stand, because I couldn't face being alone.

I would drink in my favourite bar in town, and then go on to clubs, going from one to the next looking for company, getting more and more legless till they would refuse me entry. Then sadly I'd walk the four or five miles home, arriving as the new day began. The days were easier to cope with than the nights. I wouldn't pay a bill if it meant I couldn't go out, because to stay in was agony.

Being alone in the flat made me face my feelings and deepest thoughts. I realized those feelings of being so utterly alone and unwanted were the very same feelings I'd had on the streets. On top of this I was also drinking and smoking pot, which made me feel more depressed and paranoid as well. I was getting more and more down. I remember ringing my dad once in the early hours of the morning.

Talking to Dad helped, but my parents couldn't change my mess. Why should they anyway, even if they could, after the way I'd behaved? Dad was prepared to come all the way to Southampton from Weymouth, where they now lived, but I knew that talking couldn't change the desperate reality of the pain and suffering I was going through; no one could take that away. I guess I knew the pain and suffering I in turn had inflicted on others, especially those close to me.

Everyone in my life had suffered at my hand. I decided to ring my ex-wife and say goodbye to my son. I assume they guessed what was happening because sometime later the paramedics, police and my ex-wife as well as a whole bunch of people were crashing into the flat. I had overdosed again and was close to losing consciousness.

I remember the ambulance men shouting about balance as the stretcher worked its way down the flights of stairs, but I don't remember any more.

Again my attempt to end it had failed. This time I felt totally and utterly humiliated. My desire to be the strong one, to be the winner, to come out of this divorce battle on top, to declare my ability to overcome, to show it didn't and hadn't bothered me – it was a lie, and that was now clear for all to see. I was a fake, I wasn't winning; I was dying. I wasn't the victor, I was completely and utterly crushed and defeated. It was just that I hadn't expected to be around to face the consequences and deal with the mess, but once again, I was. I can remember it was those who I thought I had driven away, those I thought hated me, those that I had stolen from, that came to see me; my brother Paul and his wife Paula came to visit. It meant so much to me. The guys from the church came too, and for a while the hospital was safe, quiet, and a refuge for me.

But of course the time came when I had to leave hospital and go back to my real life. You can't avoid the bills and the unpaid rent and still expect to keep the place you're living in. It wasn't long before the bailiffs came for the car. The community that I had become a part of came out and stood by me, and one of the biggest guys whispered, "Do you want us to let them take the car, or should we stop them?" It was a strange act of kindness, which I declined.

I lost the car – which I needed for work – and before long the bailiffs came on behalf of the council to repossess the flat. Not only that, it turned out that because my name was on the lease and I was the one working, it would be me who had to pay not only my own arrears for the period but also when my ex-wife and her lover were living there. In some ways, I was happy to hand back the keys. I didn't fight or squat or dispute, I was keen to go, really; I figured it would be a new start. The trouble was, I had nowhere to go.

Finally, I headed back to the landlord from hell; it was all I could do. I had nowhere else except the streets, and I couldn't bear the thought of that ever again.

CHAPTER 11

ESCAPE TO
THE COUNTRY

It turned out the landlord had a friend who owned a smallholding on the outskirts of Southampton. He was a lovely old guy and his son was a farrier. Between them they owned a small farmyard which they used for farrier supplies and their horses. Also on that land was a static caravan. They were looking for a new tenant and wondered if I'd like to take it on. Would I?! It was like moving from a slum to Mayfair.

This was not only my chance to really start again, it was a nice area, surrounded by open fields and animals instead of a vast concrete jungle. It was also a chance to break away from the the landlord, because his sinister presence always seemed to be lurking in the background. He always knew that if I needed money he would lend it to me, and he always had a room if I wanted one. He had lent me my whole wages, really, upfront, so at the start of every month I had nothing and had to borrow it all back from him again, allowing him to maintain control. It was an effective trick which kept me in bondage to him for years. In truth, he was a lonely guy and as such used to ensnare anyone he could, to keep them under his thumb. He was also heavily involved in the occult, which meant when you dealt with him, you always felt locked up and never alone or free to live as you wanted.

Anyway, here was the opportunity for a truly new start. By now work was going really well. I had joined and was becoming established in a small but good company near Warsash where I was living. I was working really hard, loved the challenge of my job and was constantly looking to develop faster and more efficient ways of producing drawings for the many projects I was involved with. But at the same time the company had an amazing team, we were a good bunch of friends and I loved being a part of that. It was great to belong. We would work hard, but at socials and outings we would really enjoy doing things together. I was building a life outside of my old circle of acquaintances, and that was not a bad thing.

I was great for a while, trying to live a civilized "normal" life in this very affluent area, where money and hard work seemed to be appreciated. But I couldn't hide the fact I was lonely and in pain, nor the fact that as far as my body was concerned, the only way to deal with these feelings was to drink, and to drink a lot. I would come home from work at six o'clock. By the time I went out at 7.30 I had already finished at least a half bottle and often a full one, just to feel ready to face the world. It took a while before I would be established as a local, a regular fixture in the pub a mile down the road. So I'd get tanked up before I went out, a bit of courage I suppose, then I would sit in the bar on my own or play pool continuously, drinking vodka until closing.

The thing was, the pub didn't always close officially and so there were three options – you stayed at the lock-in, ordering all your drinks before the doors shut, or you would stagger down to the local working men's club, which had an extended licence, or you'd just go to someone's house and continue drinking and smoking pot. The thing was, these were just the weekdays; come the weekend it would be worse, because the pub had a club attached and that would be open through the night. So I found myself on this cycle of finishing work, drinking, staying out all night, maybe grabbing a few hours' sleep somewhere or with someone, and then getting into work the next day and pretending I'd not just finished drinking a few hours before. I'm not sure if folks bought it, but I could do my job and loved it, so I still had a good productivity rate.

I was such a regular, it wasn't long before the landlord and landlady of the pub used to provide a Sunday dinner for me! It had become a home, really, a place where I was accepted. I felt a part of things and enjoyed the attention. Of course, the problem was a bit like when I was in hospital – people are paid to be nice. I wasn't building real friendships. That became obvious when I was buying a round – some people would suddenly appear, but I noticed they never offered to buy *me* a drink. That's not to say that I didn't make any friends at all; I had some girlfriends, but they all seemed so superficial. I guess the reality was, I was just as much addicted to alcohol as my friend Pete had been. I couldn't survive without it; it gave me strength and courage, it allowed me to live, it made the nights bearable, it was like the dark glasses on a glaring life. I needed it. But life was not all doom and gloom. I loved drinking, playing pool, and the guys I worked with were fantastic. I loved my job, drawing, being creative. I was starting to lose that rawness of pain from my marriage.

I was also addicted to relationships, I had to have them, I couldn't be alone; that meant I was rejected. I had to be dating or with someone. At the time, I was travelling to Bristol, having a relationship with my ex-wife's best friend from school. It was the one person I knew my ex would really not like me getting together with. I remember the phone call. I enjoyed the fact that my relationship with her best friend was eating away at my ex. I guess it was a relationship doomed to fail. My motives weren't pure, and we soon found other reasons not to be together. She got on with her life and I got on with mine, but I felt I'd done what I'd set out to do. Not that it gave me any particular satisfaction. Revenge is pointless. It doesn't give you back what you're trying to reclaim.

It was weird to have this imbalance between work and play. I was now a drawing office manager and earning decent money – which does not help when you have a drink and drugs problem. Work was great, but my wild nights were becoming more dangerous. I was driving back and forth to the pub and not even remembering doing so, and I had gone from being a fairly quiet and non-confrontational drunk to a much more offensive one. By this time I could drink a bottle before I went out, then stay out drinking all night. But even that wasn't always enough to make me drunk or to satisfy my need for alcohol.

One night I was talking to this girl in the pub. I'd seen her before, and I tried doing my usual alcohol-fuelled, courageous and brave approach to try to win her heart. Anyway, as she moved away and I went back to the bar, a couple of guys I knew came up to me.

"Andy," they said, "what are you doing? Do you know who that is? That's Ed's girlfriend. Man, you're dead!" Ed and his whole clan had moved down (or had apparently been evicted and sent down) from a deeply deprived area of Wales, and had taken up refuge in a house not far from where I was living – the windows had all gone, they'd smashed them up in a fit of rage over some dispute with the neighbours. Anyway, these guys were not to be messed with. The rumours abounded of quiet visits to people who'd upset them, and the pain and broken limbs which would follow. This was not good. I had disrespected Ed, I'd made approaches to his girlfriend, and the stares from the fast-approaching Ed with the words "You're ******* dead!" seemed to bear witness to the problem.

I didn't leave straight away that night. I carried on drinking, with the occasional glance towards Ed and his boys to see what they'd do. I wasn't that keen on leaving before them, and I assumed they wouldn't spill blood in the pub. Eventually they left, and I headed to my car and made a quick dash up the road. I had one mile to do, and I drove at speed. I figured the chances of the police catching me were remote, and I hoped if Ed and his gang saw me I'd be home and parked before they caught up. Anyway, I made it safely home to my caravan.

Many times I'd faced the end of my life because it had come to the point where I didn't want to carry on. Now I seemed to be under the threat of death from the hand of someone else, which seemed much worse. I think it was the fear of the unknown that was so terrifying. People often get very vocal and threatening after a drink or two, but often by the morning it's blown over. I hoped that was the case here.

A few people I'd talked to, some of the local gypsies and guys who knew the score, refused to get involved. They told me to just go, to get out of the area, to run. Funny how all my so-called friends seemed to vanish. I was back to this feeling of loneliness, of fear, of panic, of "What happens next?" Again I knew it was my fault that I'd messed up, but that wouldn't help solve this problem.. If something was going to happen, I hoped like crazy I'd still be alive because the reports I'd heard were that when these guys did you, they did you properly.

This incident didn't stop me going out, or even going to the pub. Not because I had a huge amount of courage but because the pub was the place I was known and knew people. Also, being full of vodka before I went there gave me a sense of invincibility. On top of that, I knew Ed's style would not really be to do a beating in the pub.

Time passed and I thought nothing more of the issue, but one day I was sitting at the bar, drinking, and then I looked at the landlady and she frowned.

"Are you OK?" she asked.

I stared at her and just fell backwards, the bar stool crashing across the dance floor. Then the rages and the convulsions began. I was possessed. I was fighting, attacking anyone who came near me on the floor. I remember the landlady saying, "It's Andy! He's a drinker, but he's not a troublemaker. He's not violent. Check his pockets. The police will be here soon, and I want to make sure he doesn't get into trouble."

I could hear but I couldn't respond. It was like having an angry epileptic fit. As the landlady came close, my fist connected with her jaw. I didn't care now, I was vomiting everywhere, there was broken glass and drink all over the place. People were scrambling and trying to hold me down, which made me worse. Then the police came. I fought with all my might; I punched, I kicked. It took four of them to finally subdue and overcome me. They dragged me outside and onto the ground. I started smashing my head against the concrete. They restrained me, and the four of them bound my hands and feet and put me in the van on the floor. I passed out.

I awoke some hours later. I was in a hospital bay in A and E. They had cleared it all out and I was lying on a thin mat on the floor. Sitting on my legs was a policeman; another policeman was sitting alongside my head. I was handcuffed. As I woke, both jumped.

"Hello," I said. "What's going on?"

One of the policemen laughed and said, "Crumbs, we expected

the devil himself when you came round. We've been fighting and controlling you for hours – but you seem a nice chap."

When the drugs report came back, they shared with me how lucky I was to be alive, that taking such a vast cocktail of drugs was enough to "kill an elephant". Now, I'm big, but not that big. I explained (which some believed and others didn't) that I never took anything intentionally. The police took statements and notes on the whole concoction of drugs I had been given. I knew who'd done it and I knew it was meant to kill me, but I kept quiet. I didn't want to add "grass" to my list of issues with Ed's gang. It was never meant to be a gentle warning, the dose was too big. This was meant to be lethal and it nearly had been.

The police never pressed assault charges against me for attacking them, the landlady and others, which was amazing and a huge relief. I didn't want to lose my job and the life I was building, and desperately did not want to go back inside. I was quick to get back to the pub because I wanted to see the landlady and apologize for the state of her face. She understood. She had expected an apology. I think we made up, but then again, I don't know if I was just good business. But she did try to save me from a drugs charge, as she said to me later: "I knew something was not right, the way you stared at me before you hit the ground. I knew it was drugs, not drink."

I guess I was hoping that the attempt at getting to me would not be seen as a failure by Ed's gang; hopefully they'd view it as a really good attempt, and one they should see as successful. They didn't. The word was passed to me that next time there would be no failure, and that the pain I was due would be coming my way. I knew these guys did not mess around. I was living proof that the stories I'd heard were probably true and not just the work of an overactive gangster wannabe. I had something to worry about. And, of course, it wasn't just me. My son was still very much a big part of my life and was spending the weekends with me; the farm was his favourite place. He loved coming, and the guys on the farm were great with him. He could ride bikes, ride the little Shetland ponies, but mostly he just loved (as I did) having space to play football, tennis, or just enjoy the outside world.

I couldn't mention what had happened to his mum or he wouldn't be able to come to see me any more. But I was worried he may be there if and when Ed and his boys tried to do something to me – you couldn't count on decency or compassion when you were dealing with these kind of people. I knew that because I knew how many people I had hurt without a glimmer of emotion; it just grows within you, a darker, harder shell which won't let any weakness, emotion or feeling through.

I was waiting. I had withdrawn from the pub, it was now too risky to be seen; instead I was drinking alone at home. But what a bad place to be in, a static caravan which, lovely though it was, was in the middle of a smallholding surrounded by woods. Nearby, there was a new, small estate of big four or five bedroom houses. But for the most part I was isolated in a dark and lonely yard. At night there was just one big street light further up the lane. I was a sitting duck and the enemy lived about ten minutes' walk away. I was petrified, stuck and pondering how on earth I was back in dire straits. Would my life ever even edge toward normal, or would this kind of unreal existence always be my lot?

Chapter 12

Invitation

B ang!
"What was that?"

Something on the roof of the caravan. I started panicking.

"It's them." I prepared for the door to crash in or the window to go and the gang to pile in to beat me up… but there was nothing. Just the silence.

Again, bang!

With relief, I realized it was acorns falling from the oak tree by my caravan. But every time they dropped on the roof, my heart jumped into my mouth. I became a nervous wreck waiting, watching, alert to every noise and every sound. I needed a drink, more drink. I hated being alone, but then again, I wasn't great with people, either. I decided I couldn't win.

I liked being at work; I was working long hours and I felt safe in the office. It was like a different world of normal working everyday people who just didn't seem to have the issues I did. They just went home to their loving families after their hard day at work and watched telly with their other half or children and all was well. I thought, "If only you knew what I'm facing when I leave this office."

I was sitting in the office, working, with my friend Simon. An engineer and a draughtsman worked closely on each project, working together to make sure everything was right, and the end result was as expected. I enjoyed Simon's company, we had become good friends. I knew he went to church and stuff, but that didn't bother me because I didn't have a problem with church or church people, it was God I had a problem with. I thought He was a bully, He was out of order and certainly biased towards people with money. Everyone I knew who struggled never got anything from God; I thought all He had done was take from me. I felt I'd lost my whole family to God and that I would always hate Him with a passion.

That said, I had no problem with people who didn't feel as I did, like Simon. It was amazing; he had been involved in a group of youth camps which happened every year, first in Owslebury near Winchester and then more recently in Lockery near Romsey in Hampshire. Anyway, these camps had been a great place for hundreds of young people across the region for three weeks of the summer each year. My two brothers and I had all been to these camps, some years because we wanted to and others because Mum and Dad were involved in the organization, and Dad played a part in the social organization as well. In truth, it was rather spooky to realize this common connection with a guy I never knew before and now worked with.

As we chatted, Simon threw me an invite; not a heavy one, it seemed to come from a genuine heart but without any pressure. "Look, Andy, you're only living down the road from us, from church. If you're ever bored or stuck on a Sunday night, you're welcome to come and join us."

He mentioned there was a group of young people about my age – twenties – that met and had a great time together. I smiled politely, but inside I could feel my sarcastic soul saying, "Yes, and I'd rather stick needles in my eyes than come" but I liked Simon and didn't want this to get in the way, so just said, "Thanks, we'll see."

The guys in the office knew me as a wild child, the one who went too far. If we went out it would be me dancing on the tables, or leading the way on the dance floor, or drinking stupid amounts, or basically just going way over the top. It was a bold move by Simon to offer me such an invite. Not that it mattered because I knew there was no way I would ever set foot in another church. There was no way I would give God the satisfaction of making me out to be the bad one – I knew my stuff, you see; I knew about "sin" and doing wrong stuff, and I knew that within five minutes of being in a church the guilt and the "thou shall nots" would come raining down. And for me it was the very things that fell into the "thou shall not" camp that were worth living for; they were the things that made me happy. That was why all those years ago as a child I'd decided not to follow God but the devil, because he could give me the "thou shall not" stuff. I guess I didn't want to look back to that point and see the reality of where I'd actually been and just how badly life had panned out.

It was Sunday night and I was out of drink and money. The wind was howling, it was dark, and the acorns were dropping like a mini blitz on the roof. Each one sent me jumping a foot in the air. I wanted to turn the telly up to drown out the noise, but I wanted to hear as well. I'm not sure what was better, to hear my attackers coming so I could brace myself, or to not know and just be surprised. It had been weeks but I knew that an attack was imminent; they wouldn't be silly enough to act straight away after the last one, especially as the police had their suspicions about who it was that had attacked me. I was trapped. For once I had no one to visit and no money to go to a pub with. Not only was my body screaming for drink, but it was also going through withdrawal. Having had no Dutch courage, the threat of an attack was much more frightening.

I'd been beaten up before when I was drunk, and not felt a thing – well, until the next morning, anyway. Being drunk when attacked would make the whole issue so much more acceptable. It's funny how your mind, and your mouth, play tricks; you have these conversations with yourself about what to do and what not to do. But then came the greatest of ideas. Where could I go that was free and open on a Sunday night? Where was the one place on earth I knew without doubt I would be safe from attack? Church! No one would attack someone in church. I could just sit and relax and not have to listen, but it would get me away from the caravan for the evening.

I spoke to Simon, who said he'd look out for me when I arrived because apparently this church had hundreds of people. I liked the thought of that; a big crowd. I really didn't want to do anything but hide.

So I went to church that evening. I turned up at this building which looked more like a school or a health centre than a church. The main hall where everyone met was big and new; no pews or anything, just ordinary seats and loads of people milling about and chatting and all apparently quite excited to be there. There was an air of expectancy, as if no one was really sure what would happen that night. It certainly didn't seem as if people were there under duress; they seemed to *want* to be there, which was interesting.

I met up with Simon, and he introduced me to a few people. They all seemed very friendly and quite normal. I was surprised how many young people were there; young families, people like me. The older people were definitely in the minority.

The service started, and the band began to play. I had expected church music to be organ-based – boy, was I wrong. There were bass guitars, electric guitars, drums, and it was loud. It sure surprised me because it was contemporary, it was alive, and the people were loving it. That affected me. I felt safe for the first time in ages – a very real, overwhelming feeling of warmth and safety. What particularly struck me was a sense of peace. I felt very secure, kind of hugged, embraced by being in that place; it was rather odd but not uncomfortable or weird. The service continued. People talked and spoke from the Bible, there was more singing, and before I knew it, it was finished.

I'd sat through hundreds of services as a child and young person, but it felt like this whole service had been designed for and aimed at me. It was as if God had fixed it with all these people to welcome me like royalty, and that he'd had a word with the speakers and the music group to do stuff which I needed to hear. I was completely challenged. I felt that I was on the brink of something massive; I had this overwhelming feeling that God was on my case and I was nervous, yet shaking with anticipation. It was like I was about to face God.

After the service I met with more people. I was introduced to one particularly lovely girl called Louise. I felt an instant attraction, but then I felt out of order; even in this holy place I was putting my feelings first. Anyway, I met all the guys and they were so normal and friendly, but what struck me most was they wanted nothing from me. I couldn't cope with such love, such great acceptance from people who didn't know me. It wasn't a con, it wasn't pretence to lure me into the cult – although the thought did cross my mind. But no; this was genuine, these were real people. I had known so many people over the years, so many people on the streets or in prison, plenty of them wanting to be nice or to be friends, but there was always a cost. Nothing was offered freely; they always wanted a piece of me in return. These guys seemed different. They had something I didn't. They were happy, they were content, and they seemed to have a grip on life. I certainly didn't. In fact, the cold reality was, I was trying to grab onto my life, to hold onto the last strands of it before it was completely ruined beyond repair.

There was one real upside, though. Louise and I really hit it off. She invited me round to her house where a group of them were meeting after church to catch up, have some food and hang out. I was very nervous about walking into a house full of strangers so I didn't go, but I was so pleased to be invited.

It was an odd journey home; I was not keen to arrive and kept wondering what might happen if the gang turned up. What a bizarre contrast between those guys and the ones I'd just met. But what was about to happen was beyond my wildest imagination.

CHAPTER 13

ENCOUNTER

I got back to the caravan and cautiously looked around. All seemed very quiet. What a relief; it was getting late and it was unlikely a visit would happen now. I let myself in.

For the first time in ages I wasn't drunk. I'd had no drugs and was perfectly with it. Then, as I sat down, I felt the most terrible frustrations rising within me. It was this horrible conflict between the view of God which I'd built up – one which made me feel real hate and anger and complete hostility for all He'd taken from me – and this God I'd experienced tonight through the church, the meeting and the people. It was a complete contrast, as if their God was different to mine. It's hard to remember exact words when they come from deep within your soul, but I poured out my heart and frustrations before God.

"Look, if You really are so interested in me, why is my life such a mess? If You really love me and want to be part of my life, why am I so screwed up? What have You ever done for me? I need to know if You're true, if You're right. I need to know that I can trust You, that

You're not just some figment of my imagination, and that if You exist, it's for good."

My heart just poured out questions before God. I needed to know once and for all what He was about. The tears of pain, frustration and anger fell, and I slumped down a finished wreck. My life was done. It was rock bottom again and the only way left was up or out.

Then a voice stilled my soul. It is hard to describe, but I was not afraid. It was a voice clearly speaking but in my spirit, in my heart.

"Let Me show you something. Let Me tell you something. You know the pain and agony you've had with your son, the sheer pain and agony of going to collect him from your house from the new man, the pain and agony of not being around your son all the time, the pain of being near his room when he's not there? You know that pain? Well, let Me tell you about *My* Son, about My agony and pain over My Son."

I was amazed, transfixed. I was rooted to the spot as God showed me the depth of love He had for His Son, the Lord Jesus Christ, and how He had watched as His Son was crucified on a cross – but not just that He was crucified, that was bad enough, but the fact that He died for me, willingly. That He had died to take the punishment for all the things I had ever said or done wrong, stuff that had separated me from God. He had died so that I could be free.

I couldn't believe it. I couldn't believe that anyone loved me that much. It didn't seem true. I could hear all this, but I couldn't *see* it – until suddenly a face appeared. How could I imagine this? It was not in my thinking. But suddenly there was a face; not an ordinary face – it was the most plain but striking face, the most normal but beautiful face. It was stunning because of who it was. It was the face of Jesus Christ. I don't know how I knew that, I just did.

As the face came closer to mine, really close, I realized it didn't lose focus. Usually, as you get closer to someone face to face, you lose focus. But this was just as clear right up to nose to nose. I felt the love behind the face, the sense that this act meant how close He would be to me, about how deep His love and care was for me. It was like He was becoming part of me; the love, the acceptance was overwhelming. It was like I was being hugged and approved of by God.

This was completely rocking my world. Surely this was a breakdown, a hallucination. I would have believed that but for the spiritual force that came with it. I couldn't stand under this weight of God; it was like His presence just put me on my knees and then on my face. I couldn't cope with it, it was too much. Suddenly I could see my life for what it was. I saw the selfishness, the greed, the whole focus of me, me, me. I saw the complete trap I'd fallen into, giving my life to the very opposite of all I was feeling now, this deep, deep, love, a deeper version of the same love and feelings I'd picked up from the Jesus followers at their church.

It was too real to be anything other than genuine. I also knew that because God demanded more from me, this wasn't just a lovely experience to be enjoyed and then committed to memory.

This was to be a life-changing encounter What did God want?

I always thought God wanted stuff from me; all these rules to make my life a misery and to do things for Him. Like God didn't already have enough, yet He wanted me to do this and that. But right then I realized God didn't want anything that I wouldn't have loved to have for myself. He didn't want me to do this or that; He wanted me to be me, to be free, to be alive. All He wanted from me was born out of a father's heart. It was just like when we tell our kids to do stuff because we want them to have the best they can have from their life – the demands come from a loving heart.

As I lay on the floor of my caravan I had never felt such a mix of emotions – such love, such holiness, such utter beauty and peace, all in complete contrast to what and where I was. The only way I can try to explain it is like this. It was like turning up on your wedding day, walking up the aisle in this beautiful church with lovely flowers and everyone in their best clothes; the bride is there, stunning in her white dress, beautiful, her hair glossy, her face radiant, all prepared for this day of days. And you come into the church, up to the aisle and stand next to her, wearing an old torn suit, ripped, smelling of manure, holes in your shoes, unkempt and completely soiled. That was how I felt because that's what I saw – the complete mess of my life was before me. It would be a cruel God that showed me that without offering me a way to change, without offering me a new day, a new life, a fresh start. He did.

Did I want to swap those rags for riches? Not monetary riches, this was far deeper, more important. This was riches beyond comprehension. Did I want that or to carry on with life as it was, without a hope or a future? Something within me melted my heart, my anger, my frustration; my whole twisted passion against God was changing. The hatred I'd felt towards Him was being challenged. How could He be so hateful yet so full of love? It was not possible. I realized I had seen God in the place of the devil, and the devil in the place of God. God wanted me to turn around, He wanted me to stop, He wanted me to stop living this life. He wanted me to realize I'd screwed up. I'd gone so far wrong in making selfish choices, I'd driven a wedge between God and myself. He was offering me a way back; He was offering me a reprieve. I understood there and then it wasn't because I was special or because I'd pressed the right button or said the right prayer; *this* was what the people I'd met that evening had, it was what being a Christian was all about. It had nothing to do with church or rules or doing this or that. It was about a choice. It was about a relationship.

Here, beyond belief, was God standing before me saying, "Do you want another chance? Do you want Me to wipe the slate clean, to wipe your very being clean, to end the torment, fix your mind, your body, cleanse you from the addictions, heal the scars and wounds of torment, free you from the devil's hands, free you from the hands of men? Do you want all this? It's yours. I want nothing in return that you don't want to give Me unless your heart wants to. I do this out of love, not duty – true love, which is unconditional."

I'd never met such love before and suddenly I could taste something amazing. What I could taste was freedom, life! Who in their right mind would have rejected God in that situation? I had to take him at His word, I had to see if He could really do what He said He could.

"Yes please," I said. "Yes, yes, yes. Take my life and turn it around. Make it new, make it right again. *I* can't, but I believe *You* can, or You wouldn't have just spent all that time telling me about it, and how much it cost for Your Son to die so He could take the rap for me, so that He could pay the price for all the stuff I've done wrong. Yes, please, change my heart, change my life, it's Yours."

As I said those words I felt the burden starting to lift. I felt new, I felt alive, I felt like a beautiful person, I felt free, like I had just been born, I felt my heart melting, I felt – I felt! It suddenly dawned on me I was *feeling*. How wonderful, how new. I had feelings! I felt the pain and agony of my guilt drain away. I felt a rightness between me and God. It was awesome. This was the reality of meeting God, that He changed your life.

This was a massive revelation for me. I had been convinced that going to church was about taking a sort of educated gamble with your life. You went and you pretended and you prayed and hoped that if there was a God He might show up one day. How wrong I was. God was there for humanity; in all His power and splendour

He was offering to enter into a deal with me: "I can change your life if you want."

I stood up a changed man. The voice spoke again. "Now go and share with others all I have done for you. Offer them the same." Not only had God turned my life around, He was giving me a future, too. He was going to use me to share this amazing gift with other people. I didn't know where to start, what to do, or who to tell. I knew many people would not accept that I had changed – those I'd hurt and conned in the past would not believe me. I realized that my actions would have to prove what had taken place on the inside, and I was confident that God would give me His power and strength to live this new life.

I stared out of the window. I was still waiting to be attacked, I was still an alcoholic, I was still taking drugs, I was still into all manner of evil stuff., I was still so many things, but above it all I was now something I'd never been before, a new man.

Chapter 14

My Changed Life

I slept like a baby that night. I had no fear, no worries. It was like my life had been taken away but then given back in a whole new way. I felt like a new person, complete and clean and full of joy and happiness. I felt alive – but I also realized my body was far from alive. I quickly realized I still had the same old yearnings, the old pains, the old physical stuff to plague me. That seemed odd; surely when God came along He fixed everything that day? I had wanted to wake up free from addictions, free from pain, free from all the bad stuff, or at least sheltered from it. That was not the reality. The reality was I was going to be facing some major challenges, some steep mountains ahead.

On my way to work, I noticed something. The house was empty – the house which stood for fear and oppression; the house of my enemy. The front garden was littered with rubbish and odd bits of furniture. The guys had been evicted and were on their way back to Wales. I gave the most amazed thanks to God. I must admit I did feel guilty, thinking some poor person was going to end up with these people next door. But it was the first thing I saw that made me realize I was not alone. This was about a relationship with God, not a "do this, do that", "pray this, pray that" thing; that couldn't be further from the truth. And I wondered why people spent so much time discussing evolution and whether or not there was a God, when all they had to do was simply speak with Him. Then they would clearly see.

"When you have a relationship with God," I murmured to myself, "you just know it."

But how do you tell people you've hurt that God is in your life, so it's OK? You can't, because it's not OK. You can say sorry, you can have great remorse, but that doesn't mean you can repair what has been destroyed. I sat in the car and prayed and asked God about how I should face the divide between myself and my family, my parents. I felt that my spiritual relationship with God was on the right track, but I still badly needed to mend many earthly relationships.

I began to write a letter from my heart about how I felt, about what had happened and the realization that Mum and Dad had been right about God. I posted that letter and almost sat and waited for a reply. The reply came and it was full of acceptance and love. I understood now that God was for me and had so much to offer, and I understood too just how human my parents were. I just never saw it before. Yes, the way they had shown their faith had came across in the wrong way; and yes, there had been many mistakes on each side. But how often do you hear parents say, "I never knew how to be a parent. There is no manual"? And on top of that, imagine you know this most amazing thing you want your children, your family, your partner to know, and they don't seem to want it? It must be so hard not to push it, not to get frustrated when they can't see or accept it. And I guess the deeper you love someone, the more you want them to have the best in life.

I was determined to be a part of what was going on at the church

I'd visited – Locks Heath church – and started going on Sundays to join with other people who had experienced God too. It was a different approach for me. I had misunderstood; I had always believed church was full of people who had either had their arms or conscience twisted to be there, or had just grown up as part of the process and didn't have the determination or will to grow up and live for themselves, choosing instead to hide away from the realties of the world. But now this attitude didn't seem to fit. I was confronted by people my age, people from every walk of life, and they had all experienced the life-changing Jesus. I saw it as like being a football fan and knowing the thrill of being with other fans, of sharing and talking about your team, and being around people who have the same love and passion. It's not a chore going to a football ground to be with the others. And it wasn't a chore going to church. It was full of people celebrating life, or trying to figure out where they were at and wanting what these others had. It was a place of life.

It wasn't easy, though, going from the great times at church to the reality of my life. I was far, far from holy. I was riddled with addictions and problems, and frankly I didn't know where to start. I had been invited to a midweek group which was basically a bunch of friends getting together, having some food, discussion and socializing; it was great. During one of these after-church encounters I remember Louise leaving her ski jacket in my car; at the end of the evening she'd gone home and I was left with this jacket. I was not sure what to do about it. I went to the caravan, and as I took the jacket out of the car I noticed a purse. I couldn't believe it. I didn't want this in my possession. My mind raced. I could be accused, I could lose everything, my new friends, this life I'd found. I knew I was innocent but when you live like I had, you tend to feel guilty about everything. I panicked. I didn't sleep that night. What if someone broke in and stole the purse? I would be accused. What if… What if. The next day, with great relief, I returned the coat and purse to Louise. I couldn't believe she was not bothered or fazed by it being missing – or more to the point, being with me. When I returned the jacket she invited me into her house and we talked, and I eventually plucked up the courage to ask her out. I invited her to the cinema.

Louise agreed to go out with me, which took me by surprise. She seemed way too good for me; way out of my league. I was worried almost straight away that my lifestyle would scare her off, and if that didn't, my past sure would. But we went to the pictures, and it was very different from the encounters I was used to. It was all very civilized. Usually, I'd just chased women in clubs or had relationships constructed on the back of drink-fuelled emotion. Our date was great; it was *normal*. I found I was enjoying building a relationship with someone I deeply respected; someone who, like me, had come through so much and yet everything about her said "Jesus has changed my life, it's genuine, it's real" and she lived it. We watched *Shakespeare in Love*, a great chick flick, and had a wonderful evening, until we started walking back to the car.

It suddenly dawned on me I had no idea what I should do next! Were you allowed to kiss a Christian girl? Did Jesus approve of that kind of thing? What was appropriate behaviour? I didn't want her getting the wrong idea, that I wasn't interested – but I didn't want to overstep the mark. I was worried, but as I was busy worrying, Louise turned around and kissed me. I knew from there on that this was no fluke set-up, that we were meant to be together, that our lives would not be separated, they had only just begun.

People at work were asking if I was OK as I seemed different somehow, but for all my changed life, I was still drinking. I was going back down the pub now it was safe to venture out again. It was as if two worlds were constantly colliding; but I wanted the new life, the new start. As I became closer to Louise and my other friends in the group, they tried to get me to change stuff, not out of a sense of "you must" but rather out of love, concern, and a desire for me to see victories in my life. They gently informed me that it was probably a good idea to start taxing and insuring my car. I was shocked. "Why? Do people really do that? I thought that was just rich people." No one I'd associated with had such luxuries. Could I just have one or did you really have to have both?

It was about this time that Louise stepped in and started helping me with my budget and finances. Believe me, I needed help. One day, she came to the caravan and I was too scared to tell her that the bailiffs were coming and that all my stuff was about to be taken. I hated these moments when my two lives collided, when I felt as if I couldn't live as people expected. It took a while before I realized they were *my* expectations, not other people's, and certainly not God's.

I had always lived day to day. You got what you needed for the day and faced the consequences the next day, if there were any – and generally there were! I found the drink too hard to stop. It was like the icing on the cake for a while. It was as if I had everything – this new life with God, new friends, a new social life, my work and family relationships on the mend, and on top of all that I could have the drink, drugs and dates and that recreational side of life.

People were so tolerant of me. It was one of the things that taught me about their God. They didn't condemn me or accuse me when I was a mess, when I went too far, when I abused trust, when I failed. They stood with me, not against me. It was the same feeling I got as I met with God – that "I am with you, not against you".

One of the things I was desperate for was to be able to move on from the bondage to the landlord from hell. Even though I was in this caravan, it was owned by his friend and the landlord would regularly visit and try to destroy any hope or glimmer of joy or happiness I tried to gain. I knew I needed to get out of there and I felt I was now in a position to move. The caravan held many memories of dark times, and yet I knew that my overriding memory of the place would be the day God showed up and broke my life, my heart, broke the pain, broke into the darkness.

Then some of my new friends talked about me getting a place, and told me that as drawing office manager I was earning enough money to afford a mortgage. But I could not even get credit for a phone call! I had been a thief, a con artist. I had robbed cash machines and scammed banks. I had defaulted on every loan I'd ever had. I laughed when my friends suggested getting a mortgage for a flat. I remember sitting with Louise sorting out the application form and thinking, "What a waste of time!" Still, I felt I should do it because my friends were so keen. I just thought, "From their privileged backgrounds, you probably think anyone can have a mortgage." Off went the form. I remember people praying that the underwriter would do as God wanted him to! Is that cheating the system? Anyway, imagine my complete disbelief when I got a letter saying that a mortgage had been approved.

I went out with an estate agent and they showed me a little maisonette which was perfect, with a small garden, next to some woods. It was lovely; it had a lounge, one bedroom, kitchen and bathroom. To me it was a palace. It had been on the market for a couple of hours and I was the first to see it. Straight away I said, "Yes please, this one." It took months to sort out, and periodically I would try to push this place from my mind, just knowing I wouldn't get the key, that they would suddenly realize I was not good mortgage material. Even on the day I picked up the key from the estate agents and they said it was mine I had to ask if they were sure.

"Yes," they confirmed. "It's yours."

I couldn't believe it. I had a place of my own, really mine, where I could have my son to stay. Things were getting better and better. But someone wasn't happy about my new-found freedom.

CHAPTER 15

ALL HELL
BREAKS LOOSE

It was a night after church that all hell broke loose. I had been
to a meeting and was driving home full of joy, and singing,
when I became aware of a voice – a very real, cold, mocking voice,
laughing at me: "Do you really think you can just walk away that
easily? Do you really think you're different? Do you really think
your new friends would love you so much if they knew the real
you, the black inside, the one who sold himself to me? Did you
really think I would just let you walk away? You gave your life
to me."

It was a deep crashing reality that burst my bubble in an instant.
When I'd given my life to him, the devil really had taken over. My
prayer as a kid had been heard; the destruction, the torment, the
paths that always seemed to lead to death were not chance paths.
I had been played. But then, I had given permission to have my
life taken.

There was a cold feeling of death as I drove home. It was dark,
and the fear, the oppression, the paranoia were becoming stronger.

"Did you really think you could change? Did you really think Jesus is stronger?" The taunts carried on. By the time I got home, I was a wreck. I rushed from the car to the house. As I opened the door, I realized that whatever was in the car was now very much in my house. It was like walking into a room full of people but seeing none of them.

I put my back to the wall and edged my way into the room. It was full of spirits. I moved to the phone and rang Louise.

"Lou, I know I've become a Christian and all that, but what am I supposed to do with all these spirits in my house?"

Louise rang one of the church elders who said he'd try to sort it out, but in the meantime I should pray and read my Bible. So I picked the Bible off the shelf and opened it. It was as if someone stuck needles in my eyes. The pain was excruciating and the tears flowed. I shut the book and it stopped. I opened it again, and the pain and tears returned. Obviously something didn't want me to read the Bible.

The elder had phoned two ladies who had experience in this kind of stuff. They worked as counsellors for a group called Ellel Ministries and were apparently used to this sort of thing, which was good because everyone else seemed a bit freaked out by it all. The two ladies, Florence and Pauline, turned up and they seemed so in control. Louise had arrived by now as well.

"Don't worry," said the ladies. "It's just the enemy having a go." Having a go! He was having more than a go. I don't remember much more about that night. But Louise told me later what happened.

The ladies started praying for me in the name and power of Jesus. They started talking to the spirits within me and I began to fight back, responding not with my own voice or words but with that of the enemy. Louise said it was the worst thing she'd ever seen. She had never heard real evil speak, or seen its face. She knew it wasn't me, though, it was what was inside. She later described my face as pure evil. The ladies were in control, they stood defiant as Satan threw me around, as the spirits raged. They commanded the spirits to leave me in the name of Jesus.

Before long I was cowering in the corner, torn, beaten, exhausted. All was quiet. The house seemed still and there was a sense of peace, of victory. I couldn't accept that yet. I felt so tired. This whole God and Satan thing was such a reality – not just words from a book or images of the past. This war that seemed to be raging for my life, for my soul, it was real. I knew that because I was living through it. This was no joke, this was no hallucination, this was serious, and it felt like only the beginning. It was.

It was suggested I spend some more time with these counsellors facing some of the realties of the past. They were to become, and still are, dearly loved friends because they believed in me, they believed in God, they believed in the enemy and they believed God wanted to do a lot more in me. People often say, "Why didn't he just wave his hand and fix you overnight?" but I guess He knew what I needed. He is the Father and knows what each child needs. I'm not sure I could have coped with the enormity of what needed repairing all in one go. I think that would have overwhelmed me. Also, as God worked in each part of me, my faith grew, my trust grew, and my understanding of Him grew.

The next session with the counsellors proved to be pivotal. It happened shortly after we returned from a weekend of healing ministry at Ellel's centre in Sussex. Someone had tried to pray for me there, and as he approached, I sensed a real building up of animosity and resentment and hate towards this guy just because of what he was about to do. So I told him not to pray because the devil didn't want him to.

"Don't worry," he said, taking that to mean I wanted prayer but was afraid of what the devil might do to me. But as he approached me I flew back through three or four rows of chairs. This guy could not get near me. It was instances like these that meant I knew the devil's minions had not gone; there just seemed to be so many. I found it so hard to sit in any church service now and not want to stand up and scream obscenities at the person speaking. At times I had to bite my lip to stop myself. I couldn't stand to hear the "lies" being preached from the front. My world was in turmoil. I was saved and yet the enemy still had ground.

The next session took place away from my house, with two counsellors and another friend. He was there for moral support and to encourage me, because we all sensed God wanted to undo the past.

Someone had given me a "picture" they believed God had shown them to comfort me, about how we are like a stranded and wounded beautiful bird caught in a horrendous oil slick with no way out, slowly dying. Along comes God, like the rescue boat, and lifts us out. He saves us – which was what He'd done when I'd allowed Him to take control of my life. The problem is, we are still covered in the oil, even though we're out of the slick; the oil still restricts and threatens our life. You can't jet wash a bird. You have to get swabs and water, and slowly and carefully, and with great delicacy, hand wash the oil out of the bird's wings. When the oil is gone the bird is free to fly, to live again.

I was going through the deep oil part. I told the ladies from Ellel Ministries all about my past, about deep, deep hurts and wounds which had bound me up, stuff which I never thought would ever break the surface, and as it came out it was like ropes were being loosened. That was because there were no gasps of horror, there was no disgust in people's eyes or in their hearts, there was no shame, no condemnation, just love; just a knowing nod and approval: "Yes, we've seen this all before. It's what the enemy does; it's how he traps you, it's how he destroys you. And when you think you're the worst, when the shame and disgust sets in, he has you at his mercy. For who else would want to know such a depraved creature as you?"

As the ladies prayed, so much was coming out and being dealt with, but I couldn't help feeling it was a trick, that the spirits within me were playing along so that the ladies would go away without dealing with the real issue. They asked the spirits for the names they had, and names came out but they were lies and I knew they were lies. I had little control over them at this point. Suddenly one of the ladies prayed against the liar, that the truth would come out: "Give us your name," she said. The name came out – "Apollyon" – and the ladies prayed against this spirit, commanding it to release me. As I prayed, too, I felt massive chains falling away, as if my life was being released, as if freedom was just around the corner. I could sense the restrictions being lifted in my being. Suddenly, though, it stopped, and the mood changed drastically. Instead, I saw a skeleton with a black hood hanging by a hangman's rope, the fear of death and suffering closed in, the spirits again shouting within me, "Did you really think we'd just let go?"

We continued praying long into the night, and eventually the battle was won. There was again a peace, quiet, stillness. I felt more of me was back in my control. It was an odd feeling, this freedom to manage myself. Later that night, one of the ladies rang me up. She said, "I knew that name from somewhere. I couldn't think where, and then God showed me in my Bible." The passage she read out to me was this: "They had as king over them the angel of the

Abyss, whose name in Hebrew is Abaddon, and in Greek, Apollyon"
(Revelation 9:11 NIV).

Apollyon was the angel of hell – "Destroyer". I knew he had had
control of me, but his name held no fear now. Still, the enormity
of what I had done in serving the devil was overpowering. I
had willingly given him my life. I had walked into places to
dance with the devil, and had delighted in doing so. But I never
realized the deep bondage, the deep cost of such an action. I was
being destroyed; surely that's what the Destroyer does. The very
gatekeeper of hell was within my spirit. No wonder the battle had
been long and difficult, but as far as this spirit was concerned, there
was no open door any more.

It was quite noticeable that as I dealt with some of these spiritual
aspects, the effect was visible in the physical realm. I found the need
for alcohol falling away. It's funny; it's easy to give up stuff you don't
like doing, but I was giving up stuff I liked, even though it wasn't
good for me. But the the fact was, life was good on its own; I had
something else to live for now. I found prayer actually worked;
it was quite practical. It was exhausting at times, though, and a
huge struggle to keep walking daily in the victory I knew Jesus had
won for me. I felt as if everything about me was being renewed or
changed, and at times I struggled to figure out who I actually was.
Would there be anything of me left?

It was lovely to hear during this time of renewal how many
people had been praying for me for years. Mum said she'd found
it hard, asking God, "When will it be my son's turn to find You?" It
was with great joy, she said, that she was able to share at a women's
conference how God was changing my life. Then there was the lady
who had committed to pray for me for over ten years. Just before
she died, my brother Paul was able to tell her how I'd become a
Christian, how God had saved my life. There had been so much

going on I never knew about; how many others were praying I still don't know. But what amazed me was, they thought I was worth it, and they actually believed God could conquer in a life as messed up as mine.

Thank God for people with faith.

CHAPTER 16

IN HIS HANDS

Over the years, God has turned pretend life into real life. He is always giving me more, changing me, making me new, and giving back the life that was stolen from me.

When God had spoken to me that day in the caravan, He had said, "Now go and share with others all I have done for you." It was funny, really; I had had two great hates in life, God and public speaking. It wasn't long before I was asked to stand up in church and share some of my story with the people there. That carried on, and soon I was speaking in various men's groups and pubs and other events. But I didn't just want to share my story; I wanted to talk about the God who had completely rebooted my life. I wanted to share that, and then offer what I had to others so that the power of God could begin changing their lives, too. I guess God was turning me into a preacher, and soon I was trying to speak about all He had done and the wonders of God and His Word, the Bible. But I didn't really feel I knew enough.

I was still working as a draughtsman, and Louise was working at

Southampton university as a finance officer when we both sensed a change and calling on our lives. First of all, we were called together.

I knew I was not a great catch for Louise. I had so many issues and problems. At times she had wondered where I was, only to find me down the pub, drunk. I had found it hard to reconcile my two worlds, but I also knew that I loved her.

I proposed to Louise over dinner in a restaurant, and she did eventually agree to marry me. I felt so excited that a new chapter was to begin. The future just looked so happy, and I knew I could learn to trust again because Louise was so special. God had brought us together.

She and I had an incredible wedding day. We had both been through tough previous marriages. Both of us had suffered because of adultery, and that meant we could share and understand what we both needed from this new marriage. The wedding, that June day in 2001, was wonderful, and the reception was at the same restaurant I had proposed in. Louise had even arranged a fantastic present – a personal fireworks display. As we left for our honeymoon, I knew God was going to use us as a couple to do the most amazing things for Him. As the minister said as he married us, "Our God is a God of new beginnings."

The first thing we both realized was that God was calling me to stop my work as a draughtsman and go full-time to Bible college. I knew that if God was calling me to the ministry, I would need a degree in theology.

In the Baptist church, they have a procedure for recognizing if people are right for this role in life, and then making sure individuals go through the right training. I booked in to see the minister and with great gusto expressed my aims, my desires, my thoughts about serving God in the ministry – to go and tell others, just like He had commanded me that day in the caravan.

"Brilliant, great," said the minister. "What I suggest is you go away and pray about it for a year, and if you're still as keen and feel it's right, I will recommend you." I was shocked. It was a Friday. I was expecting to go on Monday, or maybe Tuesday at the latest. I had it all worked out. I was gutted. But what he wisely knew, that I didn't, was that people often feel this sense of "I must do everything for God. I must go to some far-flung place or act in some extreme way as some sort of payback for the way God has worked in my life." He wanted me to be sure to go and pray, to seek God and talk to Him about it. I reluctantly went and did that.

But the feelings never left. In fact they got stronger, and during this time I was assessed and recommended for ministry and for college at Spurgeon's.. Life had certainly hit a peak; this was awesome. I couldn't wait to get there. It was weird to think that I, the one who had hated God so much, who could not even stand *Songs of Praise* being on in the same room as me, was going to train to be a preacher. Or so I thought.

How does a young ex-con cope with the great halls of learning and splendour, the great sweeping staircase, the grand pictures of past academics with flowing robes and mortar boards and scrolls, and this sense that this is a school for people who actually want to learn, for grown-ups? It was quite different from what I expected. I thought it would be more like church and less like school. I could understand that you need to learn things, but I just wanted to learn about how God would and could change the lives of those I met and ministered to. Perhaps the atmosphere was just a bit alien to me. I decided I would get stuck in and attack this full on, even though I was afraid, and feeling like a fish out of water.

College was in the centre of London, and I had to travel up for days at a time. I had an old MGB and it was the noisiest boneshaker going. It was my dream car, but only for short distances – driving from Southampton to London was not much fun.

I remember sitting in a tutor group on the first day at college, full of expectancy. Then I overheard the conversation flowing round the group:

"Oh no, this isn't my first degree. I have another in physics."

"Yes, I've done one in maths."

"I have a background in academia."

"Really?"

The guy next to me turned and said, brightly, "And what have you done?"

"I've done time," I replied.

You could have cut the air with a knife. I sat back in my seat and wondered whether I would really fit in here, and whether they could cope with me.

Still, I soon discovered that I loved researching and writing papers. I loved engaging at a deeper level with both theology and practice. I was so challenged; I had to look deeper at everything. I could take nothing as "gospel". I wanted to dig, to explore. It was wonderful. I felt so close to God, exploring and learning about Him, about faith, about the reality of the universe. I handed in my first paper, but I was crushed by the response. The paper came back with a suggestion that I rewrite it.

My initial fear had proved true. I didn't seem to fit in with this style of learning or the type of person that would succeed here. Then things got even worse. It was a sandwich course where you had to have a placement church, to be a "minister in training". I was not allowed to stay at my home church but there were no other churches suitable, partly because I refused to travel more than two hours from Southampton so that I could still see my son at weekends. I was called to the principal's office. I couldn't believe it, it really was like school! Anyway, I was told that because no church placement was available, I would have no option but to withdraw from the course. However, I could stay until the end of the term to gain credits towards a degree. I said no. I said I would be leaving that day.

My world had fallen apart. Not only had all that God seemed to be doing disappeared, but my hopes and dreams and all the effort and discernment that had gone into making the decision to go to college had apparently all been wrong. More than that, I felt totally crushed again – that I was not able to train on such a complex level, I couldn't get a degree in theology and would therefore not become a minister. The college was a great place with a great history, turning out great students year after year, but not me. The old sense of failure, of depression, came flooding back, as did the devil's taunts: "Did you really think you were like these people? Did you really think you had changed, that somehow you could aspire to be 'a Christian'? Look at yourself, look at them. Are you really the same, or are you just living in some pretend world, playing a game called 'religion' but not really winning at all?"

I'd managed to kick the smoking habit before going to college. I had wanted it to be an act of sacrifice, of obedience to God, but I drove out of the college, bought some fags, and lit up. I sat in the car and cried. I was confused, dazed and broken. Why had God brought me all this way, put me through all this, made me give up work, take these great steps of faith for Him, and then abandoned me at the first hurdle? How could I face my wife, now pregnant with our second child? I was such a failure. I had lost our chance of a future together in ministry. I'd hardly lasted a term; it was like my experience at Sparsholt College all over again. I cried most of the way home, staring at the road, lost; there was nothing else on the horizon.

However, almost immediately I had a letter in the post; it was from Moorlands College. It said something like this: "Dear Mr Robinson, You may remember coming to see us last year about coming to college at Moorlands. We had said no to that year but offered you a deferred place. Would you still like to take up that place in the new term?" I couldn't believe it. I'd completely forgotten about this. Because of the Baptist connection, Spurgeon's had been my church's preferred choice, but here was an opportunity to go full-time for three years, and the college was nearer to home. This seemed to be a remarkable turnaround, but a bigger surprise was in store when I went to the college for a final interview. There were people, families, youth and children all at this college; it was a family place. No one had mentioned my family before, and I wanted nothing more than to share ministry with my wife. We were a team. The whole learning structure and environment at Moorlands was much more suited to me. Here was a place that I, with all my quirks, would fit in to.

I knew I had so much to learn, and I also knew I would meet with God in this place as I served Him. It began to dawn on me that the devastation of the past few months had been in His hands after all. He had known what was round the corner, and He knew where He wanted me to be.

CHAPTER 17

"TOOLED UP" FOR GOD

As I studied, it became apparent that God was using this time at college both as a time of growth and as a time of great healing. I was struggling to fit the whole "normality" of something like college into my existence. I was grateful to have a tutor who understood me. He seemed to know the boundaries I needed, the challenges and problems I was facing. Without him, I may never have finished college. I probably would have walked out one day when it was all too hard.

Because college is tough, it challenges what you believe – but that was good. Like others from Christian homes, my faith was really my parents' faith. I had to learn to see what *I* believed, what *I* felt. It was all new. At the time, we were living in a lovely little house in a remote village just outside the New Forest. It was idyllic, but after only two months we realized we had been lied to and the landlord, now residing in Australia, had actually sold the property the day before we moved in. It meant we had to go back to Southampton and I had to travel in daily to the college in Sopley, near Christchurch.

It was just one of many hills and valleys we faced. We had no income at all, but the cost of the course and all our living expenses were met, which was a huge miracle and a testimony to the support of God, Christians, and their sacrificial giving. It wasn't easy living like that, and it certainly meant we prayed a lot even for basics.

I remember one day realizing the oil in the tank was nearly gone. It was snowing so very cold, and without oil we would have no heating or hot water. But we had no money. The oil delivery had been booked, but the money had had to be used elsewhere. Within my spirit I heard the familiar small voice of the Lord: "Go ahead, take the delivery, and pay by cheque." I was very loath to do so. I knew the money was not in the bank when I wrote that cheque, but I was certain I had heard from God. The oil was delivered as usual about seven in the morning. I wrote the cheque, and man, we prayed. The post arrived a few hours later. Incredibly, one letter contained a cheque for £10 more than the oil. We took the cheque straight down to the bank and asked for it to be put through on special clearance. At the time that was possible – but cost £10! We experienced many, many "coincidences" which always seem to happen when we trust God and walk in faith. In fact, there are no coincidences with God.

I was still fighting with the devil's oppression. Through this time he would occasionally attack, often quite out of the blue, and I was grateful for the help of wise but spiritually aware people who knew the reality of the spirit world. I was amazed by how many Christians either didn't believe in or want to engage with this stuff. They professed a faith in a spiritual God, a God of the supernatural and of almighty power, and yet when the occult or demons were mentioned they would turn pale and hide. I remember many nights lying in bed watching as what can only be described as apparitions appearing at the end of the bed, again with black hoods, or with skulls, or hanging in nooses. They would gather before me, and it felt as if I should belong with them. It was as though my attempts at death, my close calls would have seen me join this band of spirits. I prayed. They would not go. I prayed again. They still would not go.

The mind starts wondering, the enemy starts sowing doubt. "Just how big do you think your God is? Look, they aren't going. You have no power and authority over these spirits." I prayed and prayed. I prayed for hours and suddenly they were gone. They never returned.

I understood the need for me to engage with the enemy, but only in God. Over the years, He had been breaking the coils that I'd wound around myself through years of abuse, addictions, pain, through self-mutilation, through the occult. It all caused torment. God was not only releasing me, but putting wonderful things in the place of all the suffering. I was learning to use doctors, to take the medication they recommended when required, as well as embracing God's healing touch and the encouragement of people around me. It was a holistic approach that was working, restoring me to health.

At times I really struggled with college. It was a means to an end. I was impatient. I wanted to be out there doing what God wanted me to do. I wanted to change the world. I wanted people to see and have what I'd been given – life, real hope.

During the last year at college, I started exploring various opportunities for working. It was then that I was introduced to an organization called Rural Ministries which promoted church growth in rural areas. They were looking for new pastors to take positions within the rural church. I went through the selection process and was introduced to Sherborne Community Church in Dorset. We seemed to hit it off with the people there, and we really felt that God wanted us to serve Him in that place.

Then Louise reminded me of our wish list. Someone had once asked us to list what we'd really like, saying, "God knows the desires of your heart." We had put a country church, but not a village, a town, in Dorset ideally. Not old-fashioned or afraid to be modern and new. Must be fairly young and not too far from the sea. It was a perfect match.

We felt at home, and it was not long before I was being ordained and welcomed in as the minister of Sherborne Community Church. I still had a final year of college left, and realized it would be tough being a full-time student and a minister of a church, but was absolutely thrilled and delighted to finally arrive in my new post. Everything worked out well. The year flew by, and soon it was time for me to graduate.

Graduating from college in 2006 was amazing. As I stood in Christchurch Priory to receive my BA with my family around me and my wife by my side it was beyond belief. It hadn't been much more than a decade before that I was living rough, deciding each day whether to live or jack it in. Yet here I was, going through graduation. It was one of the proudest days of my life. I didn't even mind wearing the robes and mortar board and having my photo taken with the rolled-up piece of paper. It was all so overwhelming, just how much God can change a life.

The journey to arrive at this point had had many hurdles, many blessings, and many tough choices and sacrifices. But it had also proved to be a time of great learning and assurance. We were learning that it wasn't the circumstances that made the difference, it was the relationship with God that gave you power over and in situations. You could be walking in the most dangerous of places, but if God was there it didn't matter.

I was ordained in November 2006. We remained in Sherborne for a few years, building the church there and seeing God work in wonderful ways. Then, sometime later, I began to feel a recurrent pain in my chest. I'd had to deal with a lot of physical problems – some, I think, caused by the abuse to my system – but I had this recurring chest pain. I had had a virus in the past which had caused pleurisy and subsequently pericarditis; it was as if this had flared up again. I was in constant pain and it went on for months. This wasn't easy to cope with, and there was nothing anyone could do about it. It would flare up sometimes for days, other times for months, one time for over a year. The cardiologist described it as permanent heart attack pain, but with no cure. Actually, the only cure would be if the pericardium (lining around the heart) started crushing the heart; then they would have to act. Until then they would do nothing; it was too risky.

It was a hard time. I was struggling to minister and deal with this pain. It didn't seem right that God had called me to this job and then did not sort this out, give me the healing touch, get rid of it. The church prayed, people everywhere prayed. I went in and out of hospital, I cut down on work and tried to focus on other things. Eventually, as soon as it came, it went. But I felt unable to carry on working at Sherborne Community Church because of health and other matters, and so Louise and I gave notice that we were leaving the church post.

During this time of searching, my pain had gone and I assumed it was past and would not return. As we sought God about the future, Louise and I felt we were being called to go and minister elsewhere; to a church that had been struggling and had had its problems in Eastbourne, Sussex – Ceylon Place Baptist Church. The church had sold its building and was looking to move forward. What I didn't know was that God had already told the last minister that the church should merge with another. It was a tough call, but clearly from God, so we moved to Eastbourne. It was a sad and difficult time for the folks at Sherborne, for it seemed unlikely they could fund a replacement.

Still, we answered the call and served God as best we could, but I believed the Lord was calling this church to close, to merge with another local church – the very same thing the last minister had heard.

However, before things could start moving forward, I felt that pain racing through my chest again. I was hospitalized and put on stronger and stronger medicines. Eventually I could not do my job and had to resign. Again it was so tough trying to work it all out. Trying to second-guess God was exhausting. It was as if He'd brought us all the way to Eastbourne to test us; we did not understand why we'd had all the upheaval of moving home and changing schools, just for God to take us away again.

We packed up, and moved. I was ill and couldn't do anything, and the cost of removals was too much. Then the guys from the church in Locks Heath all turned up. They'd come all that way to help load the lorry with a few of the guys from the Eastbourne church. They worked tirelessly to help Louise. When we arrived in the Sherborne area, the community church turned out to help us unload the lorry and get moved in. It was hard work and had been a long day, but it was wonderful to see the church so united in helping this local charity case!

I was tired and ill for some time. The pericarditis played havoc with my attempts to work and I decided that the best course of action was to concentrate on surveying. It was the time of the Home Information Packs and energy assessments and I was qualified to do them, so I started up a small business. But I missed preaching and teaching, and before long I was doing odd weeks for the community church as well as preaching elsewhere and speaking at men's events around the region. Soon I was hankering to be back in full-time ministry.

The church at Sherborne had not found a replacement for us and I was thrilled to be able to consider the possibility of being back in the leadership role. My time away had not been wasted. The church had grown so much in terms of maturity and advancement. Louise and I had grown too in so many ways, and I was learning how God seemed to use this sickness as a real antidote to pride. It is easy to say, "I'm trusting God to speak today!" but when you physically can't get into the speaking position and have had so many drugs your mind won't settle or focus on anything – then when you say, "God, I'm trusting you to turn up or I'm sunk, "you know it's true." It does wonders for your pride, because you realize who the lifegiver is. It was a real pleasure to accept a call to return to the pastorate at Sherborne Community Church. But I had literally just signed on the dotted line when life took another unexpected turn.

I had an early morning appointment in Southampton on 6 February 2009 which meant me being on the road at 4.30 a.m., and as I headed off from Sherborne the weather was very wet. Then, as I approached Shaftesbury the rain became snow, really heavy snow – so heavy it laid on the wet roads. Within ten minutes I was driving on deep virgin snow in Shaftesbury. I was sure the best way forward was to head coastward, as Shaftesbury and Salisbury are well known for their high plains, and therefore snow. So I carefully headed off towards Blandford and the south coast.

It was a mistake. The winding downhill road was covered with snow. It was 5 a.m. and very dark. Within minutes the car veered off in a skid to the right. I fought it and brought it back to the left, meaning I then had to fight it back the other way. After swerving from left to right for I don't know how long, I realized there was a corner ahead. It was all too much. Momentum was carrying the car along sideways at about forty miles an hour. Then the vehicle flipped over, rolled on its side and then on to the roof, and over and over. I was upside down when it stopped rolling, but the vehicle was still moving. It was like a snowboard; the car slid down the hill, careering through some bushes into a ditch on the side of the road.

I kind of did this weighing up in my head: "Yes, I'm alive. Nothing seems to be bleeding, or too bad, but I'm upside down in a car, with the engine running. Quick – get out!" Movies I'd seen of cars crashing, finishing up upside down, and then exploding flashed into my mind. I clicked the seatbelt and dropped down. The car was full of bits of tree and leaves and broken glass. The radio was still on. That was comforting in a weird kind of way.

The roof had been so dented I couldn't open either the driver or passenger door. I went to crawl to the back doors. They were crumpled shut, so I tried to kick in the window. As I did that, something went "crack" and I felt nothing below my arms. My legs wouldn't work, the feeling had gone. I had no pain, nothing.

I wasn't panicking. I was just determined that I wasn't going to die in this car. I worked myself back into the front, dragging my body. I realized that the front windows were electric and would hopefully open while the engine was still on. They did. I pulled myself through, into the ditch.

I was out of the car. But it was around 5.00 a.m. on a quiet road covered in snow, still snowing incredibly hard, and I was lying next to a car that might blow up.

All of a sudden, something appeared to hit me. The lower part of my back screamed in agony. I was unable to move my body any more on my own; the pain was searing. I was slowly getting more and more covered in snow. The cold was worse than it had been on the streets. All was silent, except for the sound of the radio and the car engine.

Then I remembered I had my mobile. Amazingly it was in my pocket, not on the dashboard where it usually was. I called the emergency services and they said they were on the way. Sadly, I'd sent them to the wrong road.

I started thinking about the church; I'd just signed the contract two days before. Then, as I lay there in the ditch, feeling nothing but the pain, I was aware of one phrase: "You are a child of the King; you are a child of the King." It is so hard to describe a meeting with the Lord God Almighty, but suddenly my spirit was lifted.

"Yes," I murmured. "I'm a child of the King."

I felt God come so near at that point, He was not only there but lifted me into a place far above my earthly consciousness. The awesome thing was that God didn't take me out of the situation, He came and visited me in it. His being there lifted me above the earthly to the wonderful realms of His peace, and more to the point, His value – I felt of immense worth. I had never understood how much I meant to Him till then. I was a child of God. It was so surreal but so liberating, I felt the most privileged human being on the face of the earth at that moment. There was no one as privileged as me. Since the day I was converted, that was the best time ever with God.

Just then, a couple pulled up. They had been travelling to the airport. They found me covered in snow. This couple rang the emergency services again and directed them to the right road. Shortly afterwards, two ambulances reversed down the hill to get to the wrecked car. They seemed to spend hours getting me fixed up, and at one point the paramedic pulled a blanket over my head. "Hey!" I said. "I ain't dead yet."

"Don't worry," replied one of the ambulancemen. "I'm just protecting your face from the snow."

It took a long time to get me into the ambulance. As well as some loose teeth, I had broken my back. But somewhere in between me collapsing in the ditch and my amazing time with God, the use of my limbs had returned.

The car was a write-off. And a tree had gone right through the grille into the engine; a foot higher and it would have been through me.

I don't know what happened to my body that day – was I healed or not? – but that wasn't the important thing, because something had occurred in my heart and mind and soul. I was in love. I'd realized something of infinite value: My life is for a King. The experience taught me so much; having been so far with God, and having given so much to His work, I was beginning to feel as if I was earning His love, that I had to pay Him back for all He'd done for me. This was so far from the truth, and this incident taught me something of the Fatherhood of God. A true parent can't turn their love on and off; they love because their children are special. I learnt that day that I was special to God. Knowing this is life-changing.

The other essential realization for me was that God is not engaged in a war with the devil on some fifty-fifty odds that some you win, some you don't. The Bible talks about the finger of God being stronger than anything the devil has in his armoury (see Luke 11:20), and this has been my experience. Whatever the devil did to me God easily undid. The power of God is far greater and the devil is a defeated enemy, a spent force. The devil always promised a lot of stuff; it was like he took me to the edge of some great mountain overlooking the world, just like he did with Jesus (see Matthew 4:8) and said, "Here, you can have this and that. It's all yours. All the stuff you want is yours, as long as you give me your life and your soul." The reality was, he had – and has – nothing to give; none of it is his to give. He wants one thing – to destroy; to destroy you, to destroy life.

Many a time we realize the enemy is attacking, whether it is on a Saturday night before I'm due to speak at a meeting, or when Louise and I are praying over our children, or through the pain which comes to my heart at the most inopportune time, or through the doubts and depression that can often plague those in ministry as we fight on the front line. But it's real life; it's there for all to see, the weakness of the enemy and the power of God.

What About You?

G od is at work in the church here in Sherborne. We are just beginning to see the fulfilling of his words of prophecy and encouragement. We are realizing that we have to let God "be big", and then we will start to see people coming to Jesus and having their lives changed, just like I did. I am expecting to see many more people healed, and many more marriages repaired. I'm expecting people to find real life, forgiveness, and a fresh start.

I'm still learning, still growing. I still have to be wary of old habits, but God has replaced so much, not just with temporary fixes but with renewal – replacement parts that work for Him. It has taken ministry, counselling, hard sacrifice, prayer, miracles… the result? A new creation; a happy, fulfilled and secure version of the old me.

I still preach and speak at events, but my heart condition is permanent and irreparable; every heart beat hurts. However, I am always able to do whatever God wants me to. So often I sit in a congregation in pain and as I stand to speak, the pain goes. Others have described this as God's temporary healing; this is not cruel but wonderful, for you know you are living in the power of the Lord. That's how real it is, even this very day in my life. God doesn't always remove things; He visits us in these situations and carries us.

I've lost count of the times people have said, "Well, you know, you've been there", whether it's health and pain issues, or spiritual warfare, or battling over the power of sin. I thank God for my past, not because of the pain and suffering it caused not only to me, but to so many around me, but because of the way He has used it to help other people. I thank God, because He did promise that He would give me back the years I'd lost. That may not seem possible, but it is, because the new years He gives are so wonderful, and He uses the old ones to bring life and hope to others. It is the most amazing of experiences to see lives rebuilt, and it's an invitation that is open to all people.

The temptation is to read a story like this and say, "Well, thank goodness my life's not that bad. I don't need Jesus. I'm not in that awful state." That may be the case, but do you know in your heart that you have everything you could ever want? Do you know what it's like to be loved unconditionally? Do you know what it's like to really live, not depending on circumstance, not wondering what will happen to give you a good day or a bad day, but to know before the day arrives that it will be good, that it will be full of hope and promise, even in the darkest situations? And do you know what it's like to have life; life lived with a clean conscience, with a full heart, with a new slate, completely clean just because you asked for it? That's what Jesus offers people. Moreover, He says, "Until you've tried My life, you haven't really lived."

Don't believe the lies like I did that somehow the whole Jesus, God thing is a bad choice, and would lead to a life full of rules and regulations, of limitations and going without. It's the opposite. It's a life full of abundance, a life overflowing with joy and happiness, and it affects the relationships in our lives, too, whether with friends, with family, in our marriages, or with our children; relationships work and are far more complete when God is involved. This isn't because Christians are glowing examples of holiness and goodness, but because they have a confidence, a confidence not born out of pride or arrogance, but one given to them by God. The same God who visited me in that caravan in the middle of the field and saved me by forgiving all I had done, and changed my life forever.

God is able to understand just where you're at, because it's His desire to give you love and to change your life. What will your life count for? What is the sum of it so far? What will be left when you leave this earth? These are massive but serious questions, and I urge you to engage with them. All you have to say is, "God, here I am. Change my life."

Someone once said to me, "God says He will never let you go" and it sent me wild. But it's true. It was as if God had abandoned me, but on the contrary, I'd made a very definite decision to walk away from Him. You can do that by not acknowledging His part in your life. He never did let me go, though. I just finally decided He wanted so much more for me, and more to the point, He could deliver it.

I believe some will read this book as they struggle over the massive "when" question: "God, when will you save my son, my daughter, my partner? Lord, when?" It's something as a pastor I frequently encounter. It's something my parents battled with. In this situation, you have to pray; not just say prayers, but bang on the doors of heaven. My parents said they had to learn to trust God. God knows the person you are praying for, He loves them and wants them near to Him. Your prayers are powerful, but God is not a puppet master. He draws people to Himself, He does not drag them. His timing is perfect. But don't stop interceding; although you need to be wary of overdoing the issue, have you actually offered them salvation? Respect the answer they give you, because they are entitled to free will. We all are.

We need to pray for God to put others alongside the people we love. Sometimes family are not the best people to witness to close relatives. I can remember even at the point of conversion, the very point where I was before the living God as He offered me life, I hesitated. Why? Because I was thinking, "This will mean my parents were right." I was prepared to risk my eternal salvation over pride. It's hard to hear that you're wrong and need to change from family members, especially your partner. That's why we need to be sensitive. How did people treat you, how did they win you for the Kingdom of God? Still, it's never too late, so don't give up. My parents waited so long, but God was faithful. Also, don't be deceived by the sense that they will never accept God, that they are past saving. There is a man in the Bible called Paul; we can read about him in the book of Acts. One day he was torturing and killing Christians with a real hatred and passion to stop the church from growing, then later on he met the resurrected Jesus, and the next thing we read, he's preaching! It's often the way that those who are the most against something become the most fervent supporters. Remember, too, how God uses people. My friend Simon gave me an invitation, and it changed the course of my whole life. Imagine if he hadn't dared. Imagine if he had felt I was too far gone for God!

I wrote this book so you could see that the power of God can and will change your life. There is nothing that can stop this happening if you want it to. God promised that if we came to Him and asked, He would give us life. It may be a long road, but you will never look back. You won't look back because you will discover what it really means to live, to have real hope – not the type that is merely wishful thinking, but an assurance that your life is secure. For me, it's been a long journey, but I would do it all again. I hope my story has shown too that no one, however good or bad, is beyond the touch of Jesus Christ. When Jesus died on the cross it was for all people, not a special list or a select few. He was paying the penalty for all of us, so that when we accept His offer of salvation, we can be right with God.

How big do you think He is? What are His plans for you? Will you let Him fulfil those plans *with* you, or are you restricting Him by your lack of faith? If so, pray for more faith, pray to be a life-changer, pray to be like your God, the one who changes lives forever. And may you experience Him closely and accept all He wants to do in you from now on.

It might be that you would like to ask God to come into your life and change you. If you do, find a quiet place on your own where you will not be disturbed and try speaking to God now. Don't listen to anything telling you this is fake or rubbish – *you choose.* It's your choice, your life, no one else's! You might like to use the prayer below to help you.

God in heaven, I need You.

I struggle to grasp You and how big and great You are, but I need You. I've tried life on my own and it does not work. I feel empty, a failure, alone. I feel there must be more, that I am meant for so much more than this.

God in heaven, it feels wrong coming to talk to You, because I'm not perfect. I've done things I'm not proud of, I've hurt people, I've been hurt by people, I have messed up. I know my life is not right and I've lived it for myself, but please will You help me, because I am so sorry?

I believe You can help me, that You will come into my life

and change me. I understand You accept everyone, whatever they've done, wherever they've been. Please come into my life, so You can change it and give me a new start.

I believe I can have that new start because Jesus died and took my wrong and my shame. I believe I can go free because Jesus died for me on the cross and came back to life, conquering death. God, I want that new life now, today and forever. Please change me now and break the chains which hold me down.

God, I especially pray you will release me from… *(Ask God to help you with addictions, pain, forgiveness, anger and so on.)* I give You my life and ask You to take full control and fill me with your peace, joy and Holy Spirit from this moment on. I pray this in the name of Jesus Christ, who is God in the flesh.

Dear God, thank You for this new day. Thank You for my freedom, and help me to live for You. Thank You.

Amen.

About the Author

Andy was born in 1971. He served as a Minister after studying at Moorlands College and being ordained in 2006. Having already achieved a BA degree in applied theology he is currently studying for an MA. He's passionate about pastoral care, preaching, evangelism and seeing the power of God and the gifts of the Holy Spirit releasing people into freedom in Jesus. He is married to Louise, a primary school assistant and ministry team mate and has three children, two girls aged nine and ten, and a son from his first marriage aged eighteen. Andy currently lives in Sherborne, Dorset.

CONTACT DETAILS

If you prayed the prayer, please feel free to get in touch with us at Choice Ministries, or tell your church (if you have one). This is an awesome occasion. Well done! You have made the best choice of your life. We would love to help you live for Jesus, so please contact us for help finding a Bible, a church, or for help with your past or future as a follower of Jesus: a real Christian.

Choice Ministries
PO BOX 7758
Sherborne,
DT9 9DP

Email: hello@choiceministries.org.uk
andy@choiceministries.org.uk
website: www.choiceministries.org.uk
Phone: 0845 3888 125 (The Choice office)

We hope you enjoyed reading this
Sovereign World book.
For more details of other books
and new releases see our website:

www.sovereignworld.com

Find us on Twitter @sovereignworld

Our authors welcome your feedback on their books.
Please send your comments to our offices. You can request
to subscribe to our email and mailing list online or by writing to:

Sovereign World Ltd, PO Box 784,
Ellel, Lancaster, LA1 9DA, United Kingdom
info@sovereignworld.com

Sovereign World titles are available from
all good Christian bookshops and eBook vendors.
For information about our distributors in the UK, USA, Canada,
South Africa, Australia and Singapore, visit:
www.sovereignworld.com/trade

If you would like to help us send a copy of this book and
many other titles to needy pastors in developing countries,
please write for further information or send your gift to:

Sovereign World Trust, PO Box 777,
Tonbridge, Kent TN11 0ZS
United Kingdom
www.sovereignworldtrust.org.uk

The Sovereign World Trust is a registered charity